Fundamentals of Object Databases

Object-Oriented and Object-Relational Design

Fundamentals of Object Databases: Object-Oriented and Object-Relational Design
Suzanne W. Dietrich and Susan D. Urban

ISBN: 978-3-031-00716-3   paperback
ISBN: 978-3-031-01844-2   ebook

DOI 10.1007/978-3-031-01844-2

A Publication in the Springer series
SYNTHESIS LECTURES ON DATA MANAGEMENT

Lecture #12
Series Editor: M. Tamer Özsu, *University of Waterloo*
Series ISSN
Synthesis Lectures on Data Management
Print 2153-5418   Electronic 2153-5426

Portions of this Work are based on the book *An Advanced Course in Database Systems: Beyond Relational Databases*, published by Pearson Education, Inc., © 2005.

Synthesis Lectures on Data Management

Editor
M. Tamer Özsu, *University of Waterloo*

Synthesis Lectures on Data Management is edited by Tamer Özsu of the University of Waterloo. The series will publish 50- to 125 page publications on topics pertaining to data management. The scope will largely follow the purview of premier information and computer science conferences, such as ACM SIGMOD, VLDB, ICDE, PODS, ICDT, and ACM KDD. Potential topics include, but not are limited to: query languages, database system architectures, transaction management, data warehousing, XML and databases, data stream systems, wide scale data distribution, multimedia data management, data mining, and related subjects.

Fundamentals of Object Databases: Object-Oriented and Object-Relational Design
Suzanne W. Dietrich and Susan D. Urban
2010

Web Page Recommendation Models: Theory and Algorithms
Sule Gündüz-Ögüdücü
2010

Multidimensional Databases and Data Warehousing
Christian S. Jensen, Torben Bach Pedersen, and Christian Thomsen
2010

Database Replication
Bettina Kemme, Ricardo Jimenez Peris, and Marta Patino-Martinez
2010

Relational and XML Data Exchange
Marcelo Arenas, Pablo Barcelo, Leonid Libkin, and Filip Murlak
2010

User-Centered Data Management
Tiziana Catarci, Alan Dix, Stephen Kimani, and Giuseppe Santucci
2010

Fundamentals of Object Databases

Object-Oriented and Object-Relational Design

Suzanne W. Dietrich
Arizona State University

Susan D. Urban
Texas Tech University

SYNTHESIS LECTURES ON DATA MANAGEMENT #12

ABSTRACT

Object-oriented databases were originally developed as an alternative to relational database technology for the representation, storage, and access of non-traditional data forms that were increasingly found in advanced applications of database technology. After much debate regarding object-oriented versus relational database technology, object-oriented extensions were eventually incorporated into relational technology to create object-relational databases. Both object-oriented databases and object-relational databases, collectively known as object databases, provide inherent support for object features, such as object identity, classes, inheritance hierarchies, and associations between classes using object references.

This monograph presents the fundamentals of object databases, with a specific focus on conceptual modeling of object database designs. After an introduction to the fundamental concepts of object-oriented data, the monograph provides a review of object-oriented conceptual modeling techniques using side-by-side Enhanced Entity Relationship diagrams and Unified Modeling Language conceptual class diagrams that feature class hierarchies with specialization constraints and object associations. These object-oriented conceptual models provide the basis for introducing case studies that illustrate the use of object features within the design of object-oriented and object-relational databases. For the object-oriented database perspective, the Object Data Management Group data definition language provides a portable, language-independent specification of an object schema, together with an SQL-like object query language. LINQ (Language INtegrated Query) is presented as a case study of an object query language together with its use in the db4o open-source object-oriented database. For the object-relational perspective, the object-relational features of the SQL standard are presented together with an accompanying case study of the object-relational features of Oracle. For completeness of coverage, an appendix provides a mapping of object-oriented conceptual designs to the relational model and its associated constraints.

KEYWORDS

EER, LINQ, object databases, object-oriented databases, object-relational databases, UML

Contents

Preface

This book covers the fundamentals of object databases from a design perspective. An object database is a term used to refer collectively to object-oriented databases (OODBs) and object-relational databases (ORDBs). The reader is assumed to have familiarity with an object-oriented programming language and relational databases with SQL. After introducing the history and fundamentals of object database features, side-by-side Enhanced Entity Relationship and UML diagrams present various conceptual design issues for object-based applications, such as class hierarchies, specialization constraints, and categories. The enterprises introduced in Chapter 1 are used throughout the book to illustrate the mapping of these object models to the ODMG OODB standard in Chapter 2, the object-relational features of the SQL standard in Chapter 3, and the relational model in the Appendix.

Chapter 2 covers OODBs using the ODMG standard for describing and querying database objects. After introducing ODL, the portable, language-independent data definition language for describing object-oriented schemas, Chapter 2 illustrates how to map the conceptual designs from Chapter 1 to ODL. The ODMG standard also includes an object query language, OQL, for querying collections of objects. This coverage provides the foundation for the discussion of the Language INtegrated Query (LINQ) language as a realization of an object query language available in practice. (LINQ can also query collections of tuples and collections of XML elements, although this exposition discusses LINQ's capabilities for querying object collections.) The db4o open-source OODB is used as a case study for illustrating the storage of objects with LINQ as a query language for retrieving objects.

Chapter 3 covers ORDBs using the object-relational features of the SQL standard and a case study in Oracle. After presenting the use of constructed types from the SQL standard, such as row types and arrays, the chapter focuses on the use of User-Defined Types (UDTs). A UDT provides extensibility to the SQL pre-defined types, where the behavior of the type is defined through the use of methods. UDTs can be formed into type hierarchies that support inheritance of attributes and methods. Object references can then be used to create relationships between object types. Substitutable tables are defined to store the objects associated with a UDT and its subtypes. Techniques are also presented for mapping EER and UML schemas to the SQL object-relational data model and for maintaining the constraints of the conceptual design. The Oracle case study elaborates on object extensions to the relational model, describing user-defined types, reference types, typed tables, and table hierarchies, as well as Oracle's support for collections in the form of variable–sized arrays and nested tables.

The appendix covers the mapping of the object-oriented conceptual models to the relational data model and the intricacies of enforcing the object-based constraints within this environment.

The various approaches for representing class hierarchies as tables are presented: table for each class, table for subclasses only, and a table to represent a flattened hierarchy. This coverage forms a basis for understanding the orchestration that object relational mapping (ORM) tools provide in order to view data stored in relational tables as objects.

Suzanne W. Dietrich and Susan D. Urban
December 2010

Acknowledgments

We would like to thank, Tamer Özsu, the series editor, for his guidance. We also thank Diane Cerra with Morgan Claypool and Dr. C. L. Tondo with T&T TechWorks, Inc. for their assistance with the publishing of the book. We also want to acknowledge Mahesh Chaudhari for his feedback on various parts of the book.

Parts of this book are based on material from *An Advanced Course in Database Systems: Beyond Relational Databases* published by Prentice Hall in 2005. We would like to acknowledge the many organizations and people who assisted on that project.

The development of an advanced database course for undergraduates was funded by the National Science Foundation (DUE-9980417), and the book serves as one of the dissemination mechanisms for that work. We also appreciate the funding received from Microsoft Research and the Arizona State University (ASU) Center for Research on Education in Science, Mathematics, Engineering, and Technology (CRESMET). As part of the NSF educational grant, we held two industry workshops to guide us in the development of the topics and course materials. We appreciate the input that we received from the following industry representatives and their companies: B. N. Rao, Honeywell; Lee Gowen, American Express; Leon Guzenda, Objectivity; Gary James, Homebid; Vishu Krishnamurthy, Oracle; John Nordlinger, Microsoft; Mark Rogers, CoCreate; Jeff Smith, Honeywell; Amy Sundermier, Homebid; Roger Tomas, AG Communication Systems (now Lucent); Stephen Waters, Microsoft Research; Arleen Wiryo, Integrated Information Systems; and Cindy Wu, Honeywell. We also held a faculty development workshop as part of the NSF dissemination process, and we would like to thank the workshop participants: Karen Davis, University of Cincinnati; Don Goelman, Villanova University; Lorena Gomez, Instituto Tecnologico y de Estudios Superiores de Monterrey; Mario Guimaraes, Kennesaw State University; Patricia Hartman, Alverno College; Héctor J. Hernández, Texas Tech University; Myrtle Jonas, The University of the District of Columbia; Juan Lavariega, Instituto Tecnologico y de Estudios Superiores de Monterrey; Liz Leboffe, St. John Fisher College; Martha Myers, Kennesaw State University. We appreciate the development support that we received from various students at ASU: Shilpi Ahuja, Ingrid Biswas, Chakrapani Cherukuri, Marla Hart, Yonghyuk Kim, Ion Kyriakides, Shama Patel, Lakshmi Priya, Mathangi Ranganathan, Dan Suceava, Pablo Tapia, Ty Truong, Arleen Wiryo, Cindy Wu, Yang Xiao, Nilan Yang, and Mei Zheng. The students in the CSE 494 (Advanced Database Concepts) classes offered at ASU from spring 2000 through spring 2004 also deserve recognition for the valuable input they provided on the content, course notes, and implementation examples that accompany the book. We appreciate the thoughtful guidance provided by the reviewers: Sudarshan Chawathe, University of Maryland; Cindy Chen, University of Massachusetts-Lowell; Jeff Donahoo, Baylor University; Don Goelman, Villanova University; William I. Grosky, Wayne State University; Le

Gruenwald, University of Oklahoma; Mario Guimaraes, Kennesaw State University; Patricia Hartman, Alverno College; Héctor J. Hernández, Texas Tech University; Myrtle Jonas, University of the District of Columbia; Jeff Naughton, University of Wisconsin; Joan Peckham, University of Rhode Island; William Perrizo, North Dakota State University; Beth Plale, Indiana University; Hassan Reza, University of North Dakota; Shashi Shekhar, University of Minnesota; and Victor Vianu, University of California at San Diego.

Suzanne W. Dietrich and Susan D. Urban
December 2010

List of Figures

List of Tables

CHAPTER 1

Introduction to Object Databases

This monograph covers *object databases* (ODBs), which is a term that refers to databases with object features. Historically, object-oriented databases (OODBs) developed first as an approach to add persistence seamlessly into object-oriented programming languages (OOPLs). In response to the development of OODBs, the relational database community developed object-relational databases (ORDBs), which extend the relational data model with support for many of the similar object-oriented concepts. ORDBs blur the distinction between object-oriented and relational databases. Thus, the term object databases refers to OODBs and ORDBs collectively.

This chapter first covers a historical view of object databases, providing a context in which to understand the motivation for ODBs. The fundamental concepts of object features are then reviewed briefly, since it is assumed that the reader is familiar with an OOPL. The chapter concludes with coverage of the conceptual modeling of ODBs to provide the basis for introducing case studies that illustrate the use of object features within the design of object-oriented and object-relational databases. This design perspective emphasizes class hierarchies and the specialization constraints that need to be considered when modeling enterprises that are object-based. The constraints on the class hierarchies are presented with side-by-side Enhanced Entity-Relationship (EER) diagrams used by the database community and the Unified Modeling Language (UML) conceptual class diagrams used by software engineers. These conceptual models are used extensively in Chapters 2 and 3 to illustrate the mapping of the conceptual design of the database to its implementation data model, such as OODBs in Chapter 2 and ORDBs in Chapter 3. For completeness, Appendix A includes the mapping of EER and UML diagrams to the relational data model.

1.1   A HISTORICAL VIEW OF OBJECT DATABASES

For many years, relational database systems (RDBs) were well-suited for a wide range of business applications that effectively represented the enterprise of interest using a collection of tables. As interest in the use of database technology began to spread, relational database systems were used for a variety of new applications. These new applications included areas such as engineering design, geographic information systems, and telecommunication systems. A common characteristic of these new applications involved the use of large amounts of complex data, which is challenging to represent since the value of relational attributes are typically restricted to be simple, atomic values.

Although Appendix A illustrates how the enterprises represented by the EER and UML object-oriented conceptual data models can be mapped to the relational data model to represent the data and constraints of the underlying application, the discussion does not address whether the approaches to representing objects in a relational data model are efficient. The view of an object in the relational model requires the computation of joins over the various tables that may describe the object's properties, including the inherited ones. This join computation may require accessing multiple tables that may not be physically stored near each other on disk. In an OODB, the properties of an object are typically clustered together on disk so that when an object is retrieved, all of its properties are accessible in memory. Another efficiency concern for RDBs versus OODBs is based on the navigation of associations. In a RDB, associations are by value, requiring a join on the value given by the association. In an OODB, associations are inherently represented by object references, which are an integral component of the underlying database system. Therefore, the navigation through associations between objects may be more efficient in OODBs than the simulated navigation using joins in RDBs. Therefore, forcing such complex data into the atomic-valued requirement of the relational model may result in inefficient queries with numerous join conditions required to reconstruct complex objects.

Furthermore, these new applications often required the representation of non-traditional data forms, such as spatial, multimedia, or voice data. The relational data model, which restricted column types to be atomic values such as strings, integers, real numbers, and Boolean types, did not provide the type of extensibility needed to fully capture the data semantics of these new application domains. OODBs were developed in response to a need for managing data that did not fit well in the traditional table-oriented view of the relational model.

The development of OODBs in the mid-1980's was also influenced at the time by the growing interest in OOPLs. OOPLs such as Simula and C++ had emerged on the programming language scene, providing a new approach to software development that emphasized the use of objects, with encapsulation of object structure *and* behavior through the use of abstract data types. With similar interests in modeling complex, persistent data as objects within the database community, the merger of object-based persistent data with OOPLs provided the promise of a new database paradigm for the efficient representation of large, complex data sets together with the extensibility offered by the programming language capability of user-defined abstract data types. A major advantage of the object-based data/language merger of the OODB paradigm, however, was resolution of the *impedance mismatch* problem, thus providing seamless integration of the database with the program-ming language. The impedance mismatch problem refers to the differences that have traditionally existed between the set-oriented, declarative database approach to relational data access and the one-record-at-a-time, imperative programming language approach to data access. These different styles of data access coupled with differences in data types between the relational database sys-tem and application programming language causes data translation and conversion problems for data-intensive applications. OODBs do not suffer from the impedance mismatch problem because the computationally-complete programming language *is* the database language. Furthermore, the database and programming language data types are aligned into a consistent view of objects as instances of abstract data types. The details of OODBs are discussed in Chapter 2, describing the Object Data Management Group standard and a case study of the LINQ (Language INtegrated Query) object query language with the db4o open-source OODB.

In response to the development of OODBs, the relational database community developed ORDBs, which extend the relational data model with support for many of the similar object-oriented concepts. Object-relational features were first introduced in the SQL:1999 version of the standard. The details of ORDBs are discussed in Chapter 3, describing the object-relational features of the SQL standard along with a case study of object-relational features in Oracle.

1.2   FUNDAMENTAL CONCEPTS

The goal of an ODB is to provide support for the persistence of objects, while supporting the myriad of features expected of a database system. Some of these expected database features include: the efficient management of persistent data; transactions, concurrency and recovery control; and an ad hoc query language. The challenge for an ODB is to provide these database features in the context of the complexities introduced by object-orientation.

An *object* is an abstract concept, generally representing an entity of interest in the enterprise to be modeled by a database application. An object has *state* and *behavior*. The state of an object describes the internal structure of the object where the internal structure refers to descriptive properties of the object. Viewing a person as an object, the state of the object might contain descriptive information such as an identifier, a name, and an address. The behavior of an object is the set of *methods* that are used to create, access, and manipulate the object. A person object, for example, may have methods to create the object, to modify the object state, and to delete the object. The object may also have methods to relate the object to other objects, such as enrolling a person in a course or assigning a person to the instructor of a course. A method has a *signature* that describes the name of the method and the names and types of the method parameters. Objects having the same state and behavior are described by a *class*. A class essentially defines the type of the object where each object is viewed as an *instance* of the class. A method is a specific implementation of a method signature.

Given this fundamental definition of an object, the following object-oriented concepts are typically associated with an ODB:

- complex objects

- object identity

- encapsulation

- extensibility

- class hierarchies and inheritance

- overriding, overloading and late binding

The ability to define *complex objects* from simpler ones is an important property of object-orientation. Complex objects are defined using constructors, such as a tuple constructor that combines simple objects to create a high-level form of an object. Using an engineering design example, an airplane can be viewed as a higher level object that is constructed from lower level objects, such as the airplane body, the wings, the tail, and the engine. Each of these objects can, in turn, be complex objects that are constructed from other simple or complex objects. Other examples of constructors include collection constructors that define sets, bags or lists. Sets are unordered collections of elements without duplication. Bags are unordered collections that may contain duplicate elements. Lists are a sequenced or ordered collection of elements. A plane, for example, has two wing objects, which can be represented as a set. If the seats inside of the plane are viewed as objects, then a list can be used to represent the ordered sequence of seats. ODBs provide inherent support for the construction of complex objects.

Objects also have *object identity* through an internally assigned *object identifier (oid)*. Unlike keys in the relational model, an oid is *immutable*, which means that once an object is created, the oid remains invariant during the lifetime of the object. In contrast, the state of the object is *mutable*, meaning that the values of the properties of an object can change. The database system uses the oid for references between objects to construct complex objects. Values of properties within the state of the object are not used to uniquely identify the object in the database. Therefore, changing the value of a property of an object does not change the object's identity. This is in contrast to the relational data model, which uses the value of the attributes that form a candidate key of the table to uniquely identify a tuple in the table. If the value of the attributes that form a candidate key change in the relational data model, then every value-oriented reference to the tuple must be updated.

The term *encapsulation* refers to the ability to create a class as an abstract data type, which has an interface and an implementation. The interface defines the behavior of the abstract data type at a conceptual level. The implementation defines how this abstract behavior is realized using the programming language. Using the concept of encapsulation, the implementation of a class can change without affecting the interface that the class provides to the rest of the application. Encapsulation therefore supports an important software engineering concept of separating class specification from class implementation. ODBs support encapsulation through the specification of user-defined types.

The ability of an ODB to support encapsulation also contributes to its *extensibility*. With extensibility, there is no distinction between the usage of system-defined types versus user-defined types. In other words, users can create new types that correspond to the semantics of the application and then use these new types in the same manner as system-defined types. Extensibility is an appealing feature to non-traditional database applications that require the use of types other than the base types provided by the database management system. RDBs originally provided a system-defined table as an unordered collection of tuples of simple types, where operations on tables are theoretically captured by the relational algebra operators and pragmatically realized by SQL. OODBs provide a flexible approach to extensibility through the use of user-defined types via the OOPL.

Since the development of OODBs, RDBs and ORDBs have also been extended with the capability to define new types.

Another capability of object-orientation is the power to express *class hierarchies* and the *inheritance* of state and behavior. Later in this chapter, a review of the EER and UML object-oriented conceptual data models discusses the details of how these models support inheritance. Appendix A illustrates how the object-oriented conceptual data models can be mapped to a relational schema using tables, views and constraints to creatively capture the semantics of an object-oriented enterprise. ODBs, however, inherently support class hierarchies and inheritance as an integral component of the data definition language.

Overriding, *overloading*, and *late binding* are additional characteristics of object-orientation, which are provided by ODBs. When defining the behavior of class hierarchies, a default behavior for a method name can be specified at the superclass level and redefined with a specialized behavior for the subclass. This redefinition is known as *overriding* since the redefinition at the subclass level overrides the default behavior at the superclass level. The term *overloading* refers to a concept that allows a single class or multiple classes to have methods with the same name. The methods are distinguished by the number and types of the parameters. Overloading is used together with the concept of *late binding*, which means that the translation of an operation name to its appropriate method implementation must be resolved at run-time based on the type of an object.

The next section covers two fundamental object-oriented conceptual data models that graphically describe the data to be stored in an object database. Both the established EER diagrams used by the database community and the UML conceptual class diagrams used by software engineers provide advanced semantic modeling features that address class inheritance and constraints on subclass membership.

1.3   OBJECT-ORIENTED CONCEPTUAL MODELING

Conceptual modeling is the process of developing a semantic description of an enterprise that is to be captured in the design of an application. The Entity Relationship (ER) model has been one of the most well-known techniques associated with conceptual database design. Introduced in 1976 by Peter Chen, the ER model provides a database-independent approach to describing the entities involved in a database application, together with the relationships and constraints that exist between such entities. The ER model has evolved into the EER model, which enhances the original ER model with advanced features for conceptual modeling of class hierarchies. Introduced in the 1990s, software engineering uses UML as a visual, object-oriented modeling language to document the structural and dynamic aspects of a software system, including many types of diagrams that capture static and dynamic interactions that are inherent in software. From a database perspective, UML *class* diagrams capture the static structure of the classes and the associations between classes that are similar to entities and relationships in EER diagrams. This section first presents a brief review of the notation for EER and UML class diagrams because dialects of these models exist throughout the literature. Then the object features supported by the conceptual modeling diagrams, such as class hierarchies and specialization constraints, are described. The enterprises presented in this section are used in later chapters to illustrate how the object-based models are mapped to the implementation level.

1.3.1   REVIEW OF ER AND UML FUNDAMENTALS

An Abstract Enterprise that illustrates various features of the conceptual models is introduced to compare the terminology between ER and UML diagrams. Figure 1.1 provides an ER diagram of the Abstract Enterprise, while Figure 1.2 gives a corresponding UML diagram. The features of the conceptual models with respect to classes and associations will be discussed in terms of side-by-side diagrams that illustrate the similarity between the EER and UML features.

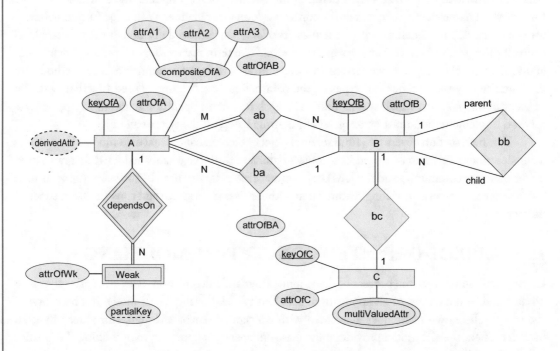

Figure 1.1: Abstract Enterprise in ER Notation with Cardinality Ratios

Figure 1.3 illustrates the class **A** that has simple attributes (keyOfA, attrOfA), a composite attribute (compositeOfA) and a derived attribute (derivedAttr). In the ER model, each entity is denoted as a rectangle, with the name of the entity, such as **A**, inside of the rectangle. The properties describing the class are enclosed in ovals and attached by a line to the entity that it describes. Attributes denoted by single ovals are single-valued attributes, indicating that only one value will be stored for the attribute. An underlined attribute name indicates the single-value or composite attribute that forms the *candidate key* of an entity, which uniquely identifies an entity instance in

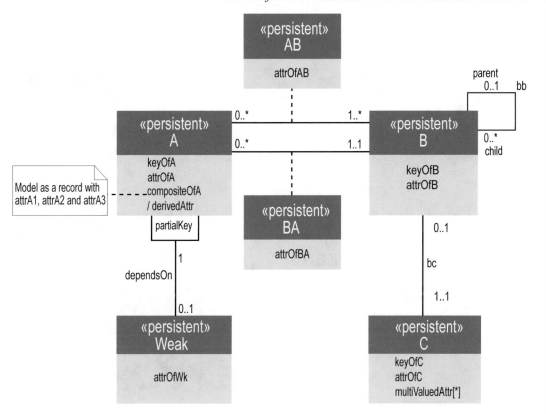

Figure 1.2: UML Class Diagram of the ABSTRACT ENTERPRISE

an entity set. A *composite* attribute has two or more single-valued attributes as subcomponents. A *derived* attribute, which is indicated by a dashed oval, represents a value that is not stored in the database but can be calculated by other stored values. In UML, a rectangle encloses the entire class. The first compartment gives the name of the class. The second component lists the names of the properties of the class. The behavior of the class is typically provided in a third component, which may be omitted for abstraction purposes as in the diagrams provided in this chapter. The persistent stereotype in guillemets ($\langle\langle\,\rangle\rangle$) above the class name identifies the class as a persistent class. A derived attribute in UML is annotated by a / preceding the attribute name. The dog-eared notes in UML are used to indicate composite attributes. There is no explicit annotation in UML for identifying candidate keys. However, the dog-eared notes can be used to indicate keys, too.

The class C shown in Figure 1.4 has simple attributes (keyOfC, attrOfC) and a multivalued attribute (multiValuedAttr). A multivalued attribute indicates that the entity can have more than one value for the attribute, where each value is of the same type. In an ER diagram, a multivalued

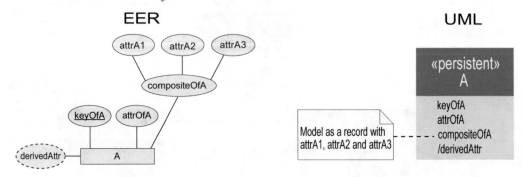

Figure 1.3: EER and UML Diagrams for Class **A** of the ABSTRACT ENTERPRISE

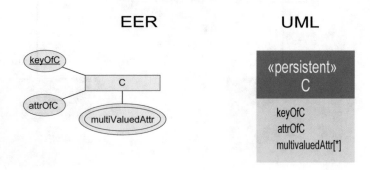

Figure 1.4: EER and UML Diagrams for Class **C** of the ABSTRACT ENTERPRISE

attribute is indicated by a double oval. In a UML diagram, a multivalued attribute is indicated by an array type property.

Interactions between classes are called *relationships* in an ER diagram and *associations* in a UML diagram. A relationship is denoted as a diamond, with lines connecting the diamond to the entities involved in the relationship. The name of the relationship appears inside of the diamond. In Figure 1.1, entities **B** and **C** are related through the **bc** relationship, while **A** and **B** are related through two separate relationships: the **ab** relationship and the **ba** relationship. The numbers indicated on the edges linking the relationship to its associated entities indicate the number of times that each entity potentially participates in the relationship. These numbers, typically indicated by 1 or N, are called *cardinality ratios*. The cardinality ratios define cardinality constraints on the number of entities that can participate in a relationship. Cardinality constraints are typically used in conjunction with *participation* constraints, which are either *partial* or *total*. Partial participation, which is denoted as a single line between a rectangle and a diamond, defines optional participation in a relationship.

Total participation, which is denoted as a double line between a rectangle and a diamond, indicates required participation in a relationship. In a UML diagram, an association is represented by a single edge linking the classes. The structural constraints on the associations are indicated by *multiplicities*, which are indicated by the *min..max* number of times that the class participates in the association.

A similar notation for providing more specific semantics on the participation constraints is available on ER diagrams using *(min, max)* pairs. Figure 1.5 shows the ABSTRACT ENTERPRISE in ER notation with (min, max) pairs. The pair labels the edge linking the entity to the relationship, indicating the *min* and *max* number of times that an entity instance participates in the relationship. The (min, max) pairs replace the use of cardinality ratios and participation constraints. A minimum value of at least one implies total or required participation in the relationship, whereas a minimum value of zero implies partial participation. This use is consistent with multiplicities in UML diagrams. One observation is that the placement of multiplicities in UML appears opposite from the placement of (min, max) pairs in the ER diagram because UML only uses an edge to represent an association. UML diagrams also provide for shorthand notations for some commonly occurring multiplicities. For example, 1 is the same as 1..1 and * is the same as 0..*.

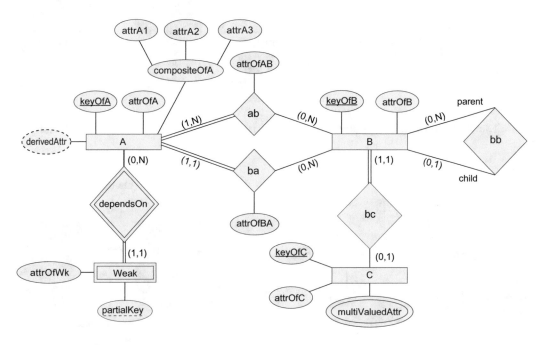

Figure 1.5: ABSTRACT ENTERPRISE in ER Notation with (Min, Max) Pairs

The ABSTRACT ENTERPRISE illustrates relationships having many-to-many, one-to-many, and one-to-one cardinality ratios. The ab association shown in Figure 1.6 represents a many-to-many relationship between classes A and B, where A has total participation in the ab relationship. An

A is related to at least one but potentially many B's, as indicated by the 1..* multiplicity on the UML diagram, and a B is related to potentially many A's, with a multiplicity of 0..*. The ba association of Figure 1.7 is an example of a one-to-many relationship between classes B and A, where A has total participation in the ba association. An A is related to exactly one B, with a 1..1 multiplicity, and a B is related to potentially many A's. The bc association shown in Figure 1.8 illustrates a one-to-one relationship between classes B and C, where B has total participation in the bc association. A B is related to exactly one C, as indicated by the 1..1 multiplicity, and a C is related to (at most) one B, as shown by the 0..1 multiplicity.

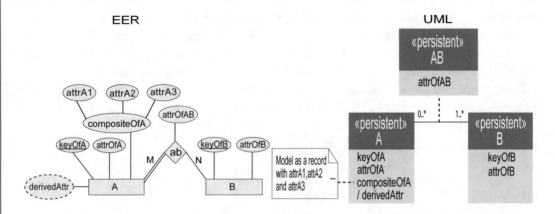

Figure 1.6: EER and UML Diagrams for M:N Association ab of the ABSTRACT ENTERPRISE

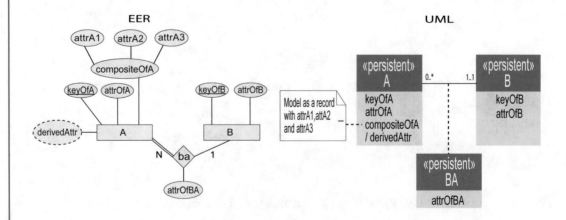

Figure 1.7: EER and UML Diagrams for 1:N Association ba of the ABSTRACT ENTERPRISE

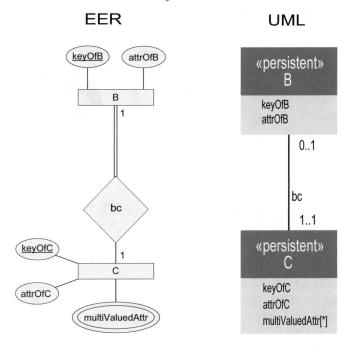

Figure 1.8: EER and UML Diagrams for 1:1 Association bc of the ABSTRACT ENTERPRISE

The ab and ba associations of Figures 1.6 and 1.7, respectively, illustrate descriptive attributes on the association itself. In an ER diagram, the attribute's oval is linked to the relationship diamond. In a UML diagram, however, descriptive attributes are represented by an *association class*. A class representing the association is created with the attributes describing the association and this association class is then linked to the association with a dashed line.

The ABSTRACT ENTERPRISE also represents a *recursive* association, in which a class has an association with itself. As an example, Figure 1.9 illustrates the bb association that is a recursive relationship on the class B. Each instance of B that participates in the relationship plays a specific *role* in the relationship. *Role names*, such as parent and child can be added as notations to associations to clarify the semantics of the relationship in both the ER and UML conceptual models. The instance of B as a parent is related to 0 or many (0..*) children, and an instance of B as a child is related to at most one (0..1) parent.

The associations that have been examined up to this point have been *binary* associations, defining a relationship between two entities. A relationship can define an *n*-ary association between several entities. Figure 1.10 illustrates a *ternary* finance relationship between three entities: Car, Person, and Bank. This association may exist in a car dealership application where a person buys a car that is financed by a particular bank. In an ER diagram, the relationship is linked to the three

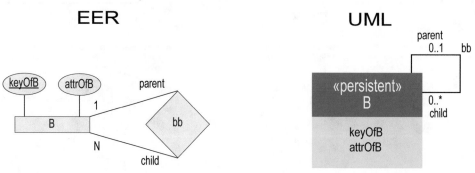

Figure 1.9: EER and UML Diagrams for the Recursive Association bb of the ABSTRACT ENTERPRISE

entities that it relates. In a UML class diagram, an n-ary association is modeled as a diamond with lines branching out to the classes involved in the association. If the association has attributes, as in the loanAmount in this example, then an association class can be attached to the diamond with a dashed line.

Determining cardinalities for a relationship that is not binary is more difficult than for a binary relationship. To determine the cardinality on the Car end of the relationship, consider how many times a specific (p, b) pair can be related to c, where c is an instance of Car, p is an instance of Person, and b is an instance of Bank. One (p, b) pair can be related to many c entities since a person can work with a specific bank to finance the purchase of many cars. A (c, b) pair, however, can be related only to one p entity, assuming that a car can only be sold and financed to one person. As a result, a 1 is placed next to the Person entity. Likewise, the 1 on the Bank end of the relationship states that a (c, p) pair can only be related to one b entity, indicating that the sale of a car to a person can be financed only by one bank. In general, the lines between an entity and a relationship in a nonbinary relationship can be labeled with a 1 to represent participation in one relationship instance or with a letter, such as M, N, or P, to represent participation in many relationship instances, creating many different relationship combinations.

A nonbinary relationship can always be modeled by introducing an entity to denote the relationship. Then a binary relationship is created for each entity involved in the n-ary relationship, linking it to the new entity. In the finance n-ary association, Finance is modeled as an entity, while Car, Person, and Bank have binary relationships with Finance. Figure 1.11 provides a view of this representation. This approach is also known as a *reified* association in UML and represents an alternative notation to the use of association classes. In a reified association, the association is modeled as a class. The process of transforming an association into a class is called *reification*. When reification is applied, something that is not usually viewed as an object in the application, such as an association between two classes, is modeled as a class.

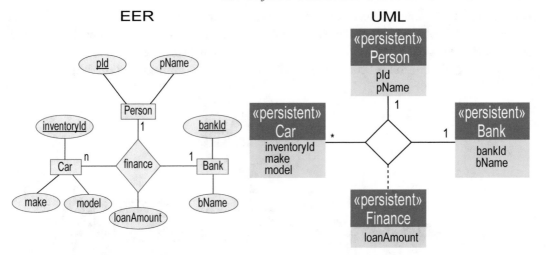

Figure 1.10: EER and UML Diagrams for the Ternary Association finance

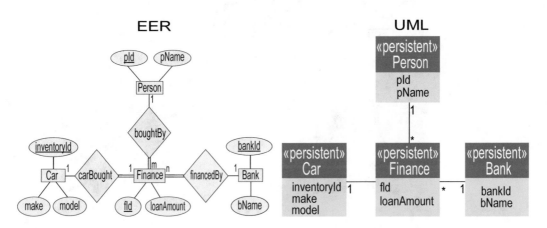

Figure 1.11: Binary Approach to Modeling the finance Relationship

The associations that have been presented so far are *bidirectional* associations. In a bidirectional association, it is assumed that the corresponding implementation of the schema will allow the user to traverse the association in either direction. ER diagrams only support bidirectional relationships. However, there is a concept of navigability of associations in UML class diagrams, allowing the designer to restrict the association to be *unidirectional*. This means that the implementation of the association is stored only in one direction. Figure 1.12 illustrates navigability in the context of the ABSTRACT ENTERPRISE where the 1:N ba association and the 1:1 bc association have been changed to be unidirectional. The ba association is unidirectional from A to B, and the bc association is unidirectional from B to C. Since the navigability of associations provides semantics for the implementation of the model, their use will be more evident in later discussions involving mapping of the object-oriented conceptual models to the various implementation data models.

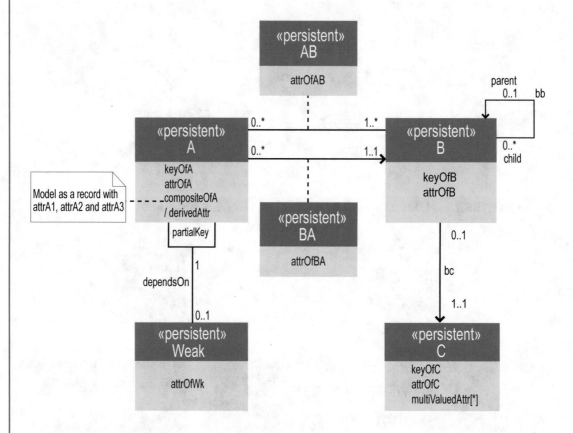

Figure 1.12: A Revised UML Diagram for the ABSTRACT ENTERPRISE Using Unidirectional Navigability

Figure 1.13 shows the weak entity, named Weak, that is denoted by a double-line rectangle in an ER diagram. The attributes of a weak entity do not uniquely identify an instance of a weak entity in the database. As a result, a weak entity participates in an *identifying* relationship with another entity, referred to as the *identifying owner* of the weak entity. The identifying relationship is denoted by a double diamond in the ER diagram, and the weak entity has total participation in the identifying relationship. A weak entity has a *partial* key, indicated by an attribute with a dashed underline. Semantically, a partial key uniquely identifies the weak entity in the context of its identifying owner. To create a candidate key for the weak entity, the partial key is combined with the primary key of its identifying owner. In Figure 1.13, Weak has total participation in the dependsOn identifying relationship, indicating that A is its identifying owner. The candidate key of Weak is the combination of keyOfA and partialKey.

In a UML diagram, there is no explicit notation for representing weak entities. However, Figure 1.13 uses a *qualified* association. The partial key is used as a *qualifier* or index indicating the one A to which the Weak class dependsOn. Given a class A and the partialKey value, there is at most one related Weak instance.

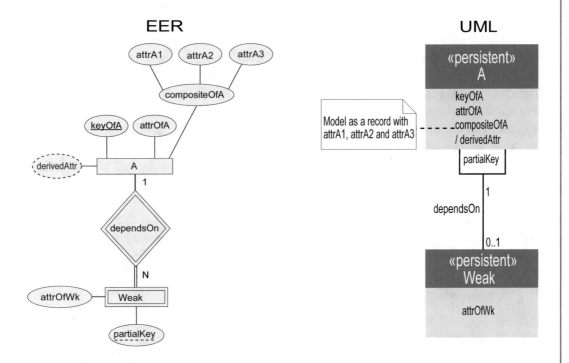

Figure 1.13: An ER Diagram for a Weak Entity and its Representation as a Qualified Association in UML

1.3.2   CLASS HIERARCHIES

EER and UML diagrams provide inherent support for modeling of classes into a hierarchical form known as a *class hierarchy* or *ISA hierarchy*. The classes can be formed into *superclasses* and *subclasses*, related through an ISA relationship. This ISA relationship is also known as *specialization* or *generalization*. Specialization emphasizes attributes and relationships of the subclasses that do not exist at the superclass level. Generalization emphasizes the common attributes and relationships of the subclasses to form a superclass.

To illustrate class hierarchies, consider a HOLLYWOOD ENTERPRISE that requires modeling information about the different types of people involved in the production and review of movie and modeling projects. In particular, this application requires capturing information about movie stars, models, agents, and movie critics. All of these different types of people have common characteristics, such as names and addresses, that need to be stored in the database. At the same time, each person type also has additional information that must be captured to describe the characteristics of their specific type of job. These different types of people involved with the Hollywood scene can be organized into a class hierarchy that emphasizes their commonalities and their differences.

Figure 1.14 presents the basic notation of the EER model for forming a class hierarchy. In this example, Person is a superclass that forms the *root class* of the hierarchy. A root class is also referred to as a *base class*. MovieProfessional and Celebrity are subclasses of Person, indicating that movie professionals and celebrities are specific types of people. This relationship is often expressed as MovieProfessional ISA Person and Celebrity ISA Person. A subclass is connected to its superclass using a line with a subset arc representing the direction of the ISA relationship. Critic and Agent are specific types of movie professionals, while MovieStar and Model are specific types of celebrities. The Celebrity class is therefore a subclass with respect to its generalization relationship to Person, but a superclass with respect to its specialization relationship to MovieStar and Model. A similar observation can be made for the MovieProfessional entity with respect to its ISA relationships with Person, Critic, and Agent.

The basic notation for the specification of a UML class hierarchy is shown in Figure 1.15. A subclass is always connected to a superclass by a line with an open arrowhead pointing to the superclass. Each superclass/subclass relationship can be drawn as a separate line as in Figure 1.15(a). As a notational convenience, several subclasses can be connected to one arrowhead, forming a tree structure as in Figure 1.15(b). There is no semantic difference between the two notations.

1.3.2.1 Constraints on Specialization

Class hierarchies can be enhanced with constraints that refine the semantics of ISA relationships. In particular, the EER model supports the specification of the *disjoint constraint* and the *completeness constraint*. The disjoint constraint indicates whether an instance of a superclass is restricted to be an instance of only one of its subclasses. If a specialization is not disjoint, then the specialization is overlapping, allowing an instance of the superclass to be an instance of more than one of its subclasses. The completeness constraint specifies whether an instance of a superclass is *required* to be an instance of at least one of its subclasses, which is referred to as a *total specialization*. Otherwise, the specialization is a *partial specialization*. A total specialization is also referred to as a *covering constraint*. Disjoint and completeness constraints can be used together to form the semantics of subclass membership with respect to the superclass.

Figure 1.16 illustrates the notational conventions for disjoint and completeness constraints. As shown in Figure 1.16(a), A has a disjoint specialization into its subclasses B and C, which is indicated by the use of a circle enclosing the letter "d" within the ISA specification. As a result, taking the

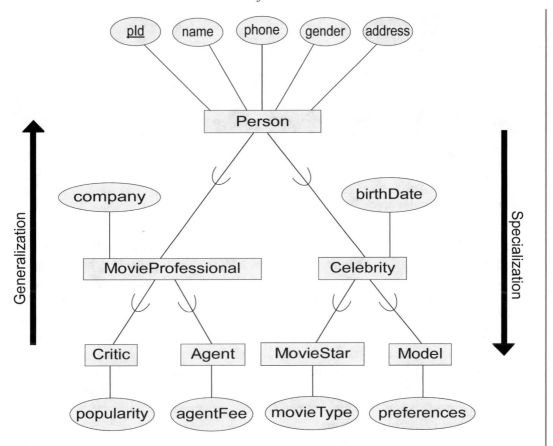

Figure 1.14: Generalization and Specialization in the **Person** Class Hierarchy. Based on "Database Models," by S. Urban in *Encyclopedia of Electrical and Electronics Engineering*, John G. Webster (editor); Copyright ©1999 John G. Webster. This material is used by permission of John Wiley & Sons, Inc.

intersection of the instances of **B** and **C** should yield the empty set, indicating that an instance of **A** can either be an instance of **B** or an instance of **C**, but not an instance of both **B** and **C**. If subclasses are not disjoint, then they are overlapping, meaning that an entity can be an instance of multiple subclasses. The notation for the specification of overlapping subclass membership is indicated in Figure 1.16(b), using a circle to enclose the letter "o". Since **D** has an overlapping specialization into its subclasses **E** and **F**, an entity can be an instance of **E** and **F** at the same time. The notation used to introduce EER class hierarchies in Figure 1.14 is, by default, assumed to represent overlapping subclass membership.

The notation for indicating the completeness constraint in the EER is consistent with ER modeling notation for participation constraints. A total specialization indicates total participation

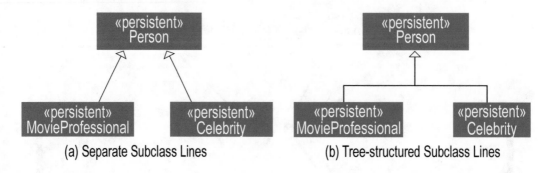

Figure 1.15: Notation for Specialization in UML

of the superclass in the specialization relationship, which is denoted by a double line connecting the superclass to the specialization circle. In Figure 1.16(c), an entity cannot exist as an instance of A without also being an instance of either B or C. This implies that at the time an instance of A is created, the specific subclass or subclasses to which it belongs must also be specified. Partial specialization indicates partial participation in the specialization relationship, which is denoted by a single line connecting the superclass to the specialization circle. In Figure 1.16(d), an instance of D is not required to be an instance of E or F. By default, the single lines used in the notational convention of Figure 1.14 also indicate partial specialization. For Figures 1.16(c) and Figure 1.16(d), the circle can be filled with either a "d" or an "o" to indicate the disjoint or overlapping constraint, respectively, creating four possibilities for specialization constraints: total disjoint, partial disjoint, total overlapping, or partial overlapping.

Figure 1.17 presents a revised version of Figure 1.14, adding disjoint and completeness constraints. As indicated in Figure 1.17, a Person is not required to be a MovieProfessional or a Celebrity. When an instance of Person does exist at the subclass level, the Person instance cannot be both a Celebrity and a MovieProfessional at the same time. Since Celebrity has a total participation constraint with its subclasses, creating a Celebrity instance also requires the creation of a MovieStar or Model instance. Furthermore, since MovieStar and Model are overlapping, a celebrity can be an instance of both subclasses. MovieProfessional also has total participation with its subclasses. Membership in the Critic and Agent classes, however, is disjoint.

The UML notation for specialization constraints are explicit constraint names that are enclosed in braces ({}) and attached to the specialization link between a subclass and a superclass. The disjoint constraint specifies that the intersection of a set of subclasses must be the empty set. In other words, an instance of the superclass can only be an instance of one of the subclasses. The overlapping constraint indicates that an instance of the superclass can be an instance of multiple subclasses. When there is no explicit specialization constraint given in the UML diagram, as in Figure 1.15, the default constraint is disjoint subclass membership. The complete and incomplete constraints specify whether all of the subclasses have been shown in the class hierarchy, where complete indicates that

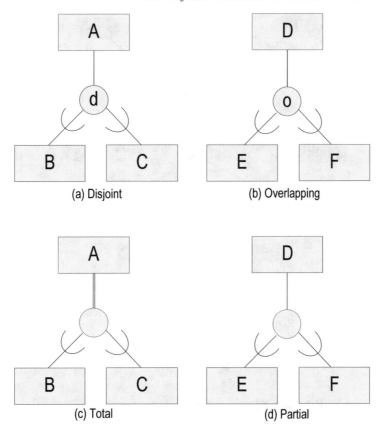

Figure 1.16: EER Notation for Disjoint and Completeness Constraints

there are no more subclasses to define and incomplete indicates that all of the subclasses have not yet been indicated in the diagram. These constraints (disjoint, overlapping, complete, and incomplete) are UML-defined constraints. An additional mandatory user-defined constraint, introduced for the purpose of database modeling, specifies that each instance of the superclass is required to be an instance of at least one of its subclasses.

The UML version of the Person class hierarchy from Figure 1.17 is shown in Figure 1.18. At each level of the hierarchy, specific constraints are attached to each specialization tree. According to the constraints, an instance of Person can be an instance of MovieProfessional or Celebrity, but not both. Since a mandatory constraint was not specified, a Person instance is not required to exist at the subclass level. For the specialization of MovieProfessional, participation at the subclass level is disjoint and mandatory. Insertion of an instance in the MovieProfessional class therefore implies the required insertion of the instance into either Critic or Agent. Because of the overlapping

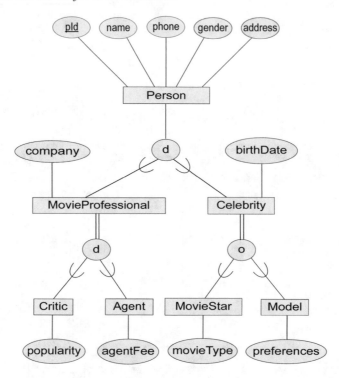

Figure 1.17: Revised EER **Person** Hierarchy with Disjoint and Completeness Constraints. Based on "Database Models," by S. Urban in *Encyclopedia of Electrical and Electronics Engineering*, John G. Webster (editor); Copyright ©1999 John G. Webster. This material is used by permission of John Wiley & Sons, Inc.

and **mandatory** constraints on the **Celebrity** specialization, an instance of **Celebrity** is required to participate at the subclass level and can be a movie star *and* a model at the same time. Note that the **overlapping** and **disjoint** constraints are identical to the corresponding constraints in the EER model. The **mandatory** constraint corresponds to the completeness constraint of the EER model, indicating total specialization. The absence of the **mandatory** constraint corresponds to partial specialization.

1.3.2.2 Attribute-Defined Specialization

The forms of specialization that have been examined so far are examples of *user-defined specialization*. In user-defined specialization, it is up to the application user to determine the subclass or subclasses to which a superclass instance can belong. Another form of specialization is *attribute-defined special-ization*, where the value of an attribute at the superclass level determines membership in a subclass. Figure 1.19 presents an example of attribute-defined specialization in the EER model. In this ex-

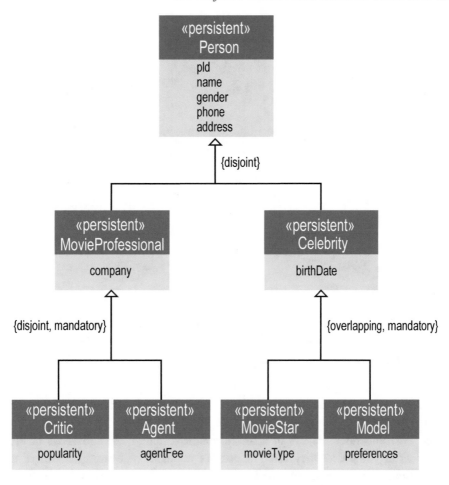

Figure 1.18: UML Specialization Constraints on the Person Hierarchy

ample, the Project class is specialized into the FilmProject class and the ModelingProject class based on the value of the type attribute of Project being either "F" or "M".

As in the EER model, UML supports membership in subclasses based on the value of an attribute at the superlass level. The attribute that determines subclass membership is referred to as a *discriminator*. The use of a discriminator in UML always implies disjoint and mandatory subclass membership. Furthermore, a subclass must exist for all possible values of the discriminator.

A discriminator is specified as a label on the specialization link and is considered to be a *pseudoattribute* of the superclass. A pseudoattribute behaves like a regular class attribute except that

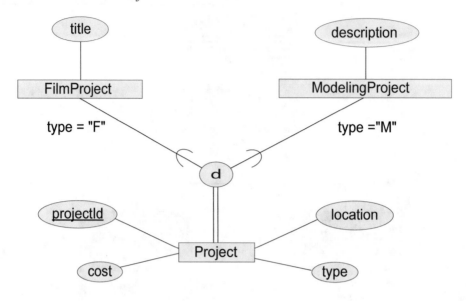

Figure 1.19: The Project Attribute-Defined Specialization in an EER Diagram. Based on "Database Models," by S. Urban in *Encyclopedia of Electrical and Electronics Engineering*, John G. Webster (editor); Copyright ©1999 John G. Webster. This material is used by permission of John Wiley & Sons, Inc.

the domain of the attribute is the set of subclass names. A pseudoattribute does not appear in the attribute compartment of a class definition.

Figure 1.20 illustrates the use of a discriminator to define the subclasses of Project. The discriminator is the type pseudoattribute. The possible values for type are "FilmProject" and "ModelingProject". Because a discriminator implies mandatory subclass membership, the Project class is an *abstract class*, illustrated with the name of the class in italics. An abstract class is a class that cannot be directly instantiated. In Figure 1.20, a Project object can only be created either as an instance of FilmProject or as an instance of ModelingProject. Because of the ISA constraint, the object is automatically an instance of Project. At the Project level, the object has a type attribute that indicates the subclass to which the object belongs.

1.3.2.3 Multiple Inheritance

Each example presented so far has illustrated the use of a *specialization hierarchy*, where each subclass has only one superclass. In some modeling situations, it is possible for a subclass to have more than one superclass, thus forming a *specialization lattice*. In a specialization lattice, a class with more than one superclass is referred to as a *shared subclass*.

A shared subclass supports *multiple inheritance*, where the subclass inherits attributes from *all* of its superclasses. A shared subclass must satisfy the *multiple inheritance intersection constraint*,

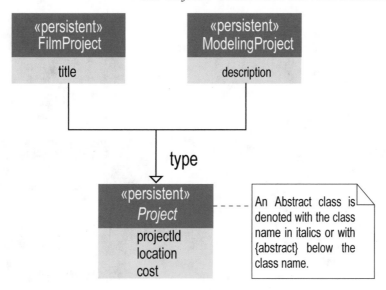

Figure 1.20: Use of a Discriminator for **Project** Specialization in a UML Diagram

where the entity set of the subclass represents the *intersection* of the superclasses in the lattice. In other words, an entity can only be an instance of a shared subclass if it is an instance of all of its superclasses.

In Figure 1.21, StarModel is a shared subclass with MovieStar and Model as superclasses. The StarModel class therefore contains instances that are both movie stars and models. Each instance of StarModel inherits attributes from MovieStar, Model, and Celebrity. One of the problems with multiple inheritance is that each superclass can have attributes with the same name, thus creating ambiguity in the inheritance process. If the application designer decides to use multiple inheritance, the designer should ensure that the names of all inherited attributes are unique.

The superclasses of a shared subclass must have a common ancestor. The common ancestor ensures that instances of the shared subclass are of the same fundamental type of entity. In the StarModel shared subclass, the Person class is a common ancestor, allowing the system to create only one copy of the common attributes. A class that has multiple superclasses that *do not* have a common ancestor can be modeled using the category feature of the EER model or an XOR association constraint in UML described in the next section.

1.3.3   CATEGORIES AND XOR ASSOCIATION CONSTRAINT

Whereas multiple inheritance is used to model the intersection of two subclasses with a common root class, a *category* is used to model the *union* of two or more different types of classes. A category therefore represents a heterogeneous collection of entity instances, unlike other classes which are

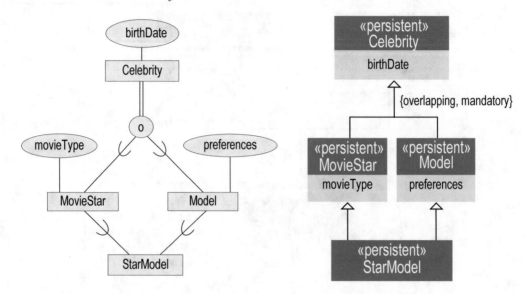

Figure 1.21: The StarModel Shared Subclass. Based on "Database Models," by S. Urban in *Encyclopedia of Electrical and Electronics Engineering*, John G. Webster (editor); Copyright ©1999 John G. Webster. This material is used by permission of John Wiley & Sons, Inc.

homogeneous collections. An instance of a category subclass must be an instance of at least one of its superclasses but may not necessarily be a member of all of its superclasses.

Figure 1.22 illustrates the notational convention for categories together with the different types of constraints on categorization. In general, the superclasses of a category are connected by a single line to a union symbol enclosed in a circle. The circle is then connected by a line to the category subclass. A union symbol on the line indicates the direction of the union relationship.

Categories must satisfy either the *total category constraint* or *partial category constraint*. A total categorization is depicted in Figure 1.22(a) with a double line between the subclass and the circle. If a category is constrained to be total, then every instance of each superclass must participate in the categorization and be an instance of the category subclass. To satisfy the total category constraint, a category must therefore be equal to the union of it superclasses. Partial categorization is shown in Figure 1.22(b) with a single line between the subclass and the circle. If a category is partial, then an instance of a superclass is not required to participate in the categorization and need not be an instance of the category subclass. To satisfy the partial category constraint, the category must be a subset of the union of its superclasses.

Figure 1.23 illustrates the use of categorization in the HOLLYWOOD ENTERPRISE. In particular, either a person or a company can sponsor a modeling project. Instead of creating two separate sponsor relationships between Person and ModelingProject and between Company and Modeling-

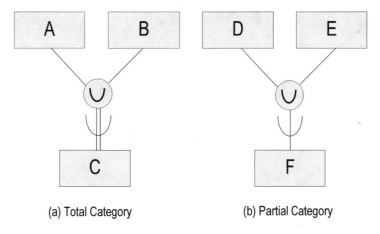

(a) Total Category   (b) Partial Category

Figure 1.22: EER Notation for Total and Partial Categories

Project, it is useful to define the notion of a sponsor as a category, where a Sponsor class is a subset of the union of the Person and Company classes. A sponsoredBy relationship is then defined once between the Sponsor class and the ModelingProject class. The Sponsor class is defined as a partial category to indicate that every person instance and every company instance is not required to be a sponsor. On the other hand, an instance of the Sponsor class represents an entity that is either a Person instance *or* a Company instance, but *not* an instance of both the Person *and* Company classes, as in the case of multiple inheritance and shared subclasses.

Categories from the EER model can be represented using the *xor constraint* on associations in UML class diagrams, which indicates that, at any given time, the application only needs to use one of the associations. To illustrate this point, Figure 1.24 shows the Sponsor, Person, and Company classes with two associations, one between Sponsor and Person and another between Sponsor and Company. Sponsor is referred to as the *base class*. An xor constraint is specified between the two associations, drawn as a dashed line labeled with {xor}, indicating that a sponsor object can be related to one person object or one company object, but not both. The multiplicity on the Person and Company side of each association is 1, indicating that every instance of Sponsor is *required* to be related to either a person or a company. In the opposite direction, the multiplicity specified can be used to indicate total or partial participation of Person and Company objects with Sponsor objects. In Figure 1.24, the multiplicity for each association is 0..1, indicating that each Person object and each Company object does not have to be related to a Sponsor object, thus capturing the notion of a partial category from the EER model. The multiplicity can be changed to 1..1 on each association to represent the concept of a total category, meaning that every person and every company is related to its corresponding Sponsor object.

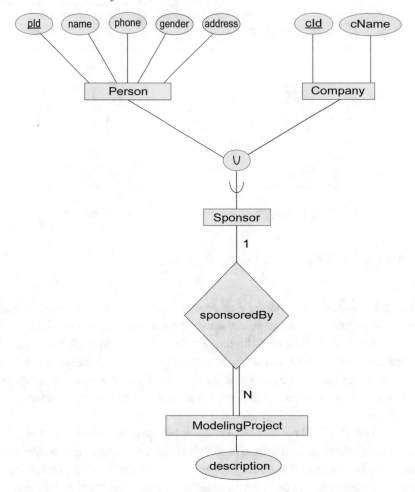

Figure 1.23: The Sponsor Partial Category. Based on "Database Models," by S. Urban in *Encyclopedia of Electrical and Electronics Engineering*, John G. Webster (editor); Copyright ©1999 John G. Webster. This material is used by permission of John Wiley & Sons, Inc.

1.3.4   CHECKPOINT: EER AND UML

This section has presented the similar modeling capabilities of the EER and UML conceptual data models using side-by-side illustrations, capturing classes, associations, class hierarchies with specializations constraints, and categories. The complete conceptual design of the HOLLYWOOD ENTERPRISE is presented in Figure 1.25 as an EER diagram and in Figure 1.26 as a UML class diagram.

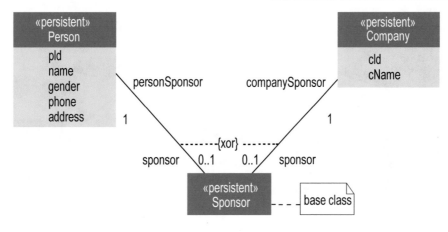

Figure 1.24: Using an Xor Constraint to Model the Partial `Sponsor` Category

1.4   BIBLIOGRAPHIC REFERENCES

Initially, characterizing OODB technology was complicated by the fact that many commercial OODB products were developed before the existence of any common, formal definition of an OODB model. This is contrary to RDB technology, in which commercial development followed a clear, formal definition of the relational data model. The *Object-Oriented Database System Manifesto* [Atkinson et al., 1990] is generally considered to be the most definitive summary of OODB characteristics, with numerous other research papers providing more formal definitions of object-oriented data models. The research paper [Koshafian and Copeland, 1989] provides a formal definition of object identity.

Seminal work on the ER model appeared in [Chen, 1976]. Although there are several different notational variations of the EER model, our presentation is based on the work in [Elmasri and Navathe, 2010]. Foundational data modeling issues for Elmasri's version of the EER model were originally addressed in [Wiederhold and Elmasri, 1979], with structural constraints defined in [Elmasri and Wiederhold, 1980] and categories introduced in [Elmasri et al., 1985]. The EER model is based on concepts that originated with research on semantic data modeling. The concepts of generalization and specialization in semantic data models originated with the work of [Smith and Smith, 1977]. Excellent surveys of the semantic modeling concepts that have influenced the design of the EER model can be found in [Hull and King, 1987] and [Peckham and Maryanski, 1988].

The development of UML was inspired by the introduction of object-oriented programming languages and object-oriented design techniques. Although Simula-67 [Dahl et al., 1967] is generally regarded as the first object-oriented programming language, most object-oriented languages, such as Smalltalk [Goldberg and Robson, 1983], C++ [Stroustrup, 1986], and Eiffel [Meyer, 1988],

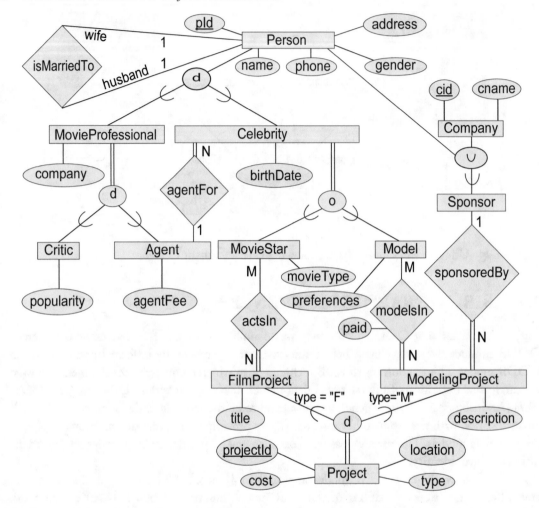

Figure 1.25: EER Diagram of the HOLLYWOOD ENTERPRISE. Based on "Database Models," by S. Urban in *Encyclopedia of Electrical and Electronics Engineering*, John G. Webster (editor); Copyright ©1999 John G. Webster. This material is used by permission of John Wiley & Sons, Inc.

did not become popular until the early 1980's. More recent definitions of object-oriented programming languages appear in the descriptions of C++ [Stroustrup, 2000] and Java [Arnold et al., 2005]. Widespread interest in object-oriented programming languages was followed by research involving the development of object-oriented design techniques, the most prevalent of which were James Rumbaugh's Object Management Technique [Rumbaugh et al., 1991], Ivar Jacobson's Object-Oriented Software Engineering Notation [Jacobson et al., 1992], and Grady Booch's Object-Oriented Anal-

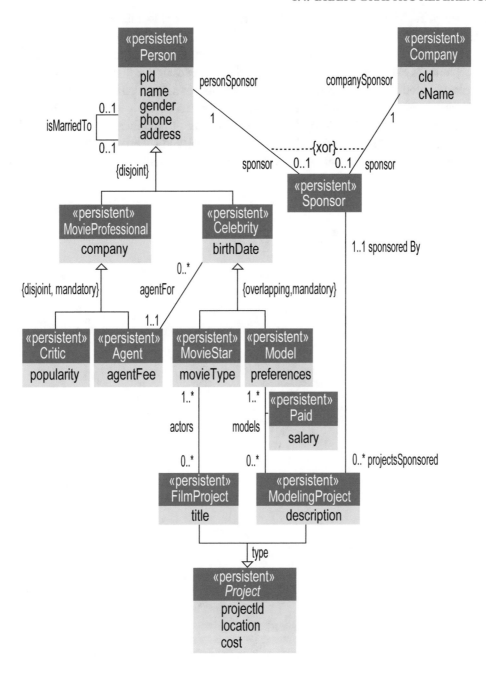

Figure 1.26: UML Class Diagram of the HOLLYWOOD ENTERPRISE

ysis and Design Technique [Booch, 1994]. Eventually, the work of Rumbaugh, Jacobson, and Booch converged when all three joined the Rational Software Corporation in the mid 1990's, leading to the creation of UML. In 1996, the specification of UML was submitted to the Object Management Group (OMG) in response to a request for proposals for a standardized approach to object-oriented modeling. UML was subsequently adopted as a standard by the OMG in 1997 and has continued to evolve since that time. The specification of UML is maintained by OMG and can be found at [OMG-UML, 2010]. Other useful sources of reference for UML class diagrams are [Rumbaugh et al., 2004], [Fowler, 2003], [Muller, 1999], and [Schmuller, 2004].

The HOLLYWOOD ENTERPRISE used in this chapter originally appeared in an encyclopedia article on data modeling [Urban, 1999].

CHAPTER 2

Object-Oriented Databases

The OODB community developed the Object Data Management Group (ODMG) standard as a means of establishing a common object interface specification to promote portability among commercial OODB products. The ODMG data model is based on the data model of the Object Management Group (OMG) standard, which provides object-oriented interface capabilities for interoperability across applications. The database designer uses the Object Definition Language (ODL) of the ODMG standard to specify the object types in the application according to the ODMG object model, which is independent of a particular database or vendor. This chapter begins with coverage of the ODMG object model and definition language, and then details the mapping of the EER and UML object-oriented conceptual data models to the ODL. Once the schema is defined in the ODL, the Object Query Language (OQL) of the ODMG standard provides a declarative language for querying the database. OQL contributes a test bed for the study of query optimization techniques for object databases and a database independent way to describe declarative queries over the ODMG object model. Today, the recently introduced Language INtegrated Query (LINQ) language provides a declarative query language for OODBs. The chapter concludes with a case study using the db4o open-source OODB with LINQ as the declarative query language.

2.1 THE ODMG STANDARD

Unlike the relational data model, which was introduced theoretically before the implementation of commercial relational database products, the object-oriented data model evolved by adding the capability of persistence to objects in an object-oriented programming language. Several object-oriented database products emerged before the development of the ODMG Standard. The standard provides a common ground to describe an object model, the specification of a schema over the object model, and a query language. The standard also specifies language bindings for C++, Smalltalk, and Java. Language bindings are libraries of classes and functions that implement the concepts for the definition and manipulation of objects based on the standard in the given OOPL.

The modeling primitives of the ODMG standard are objects and literals. Objects have object identifiers. Literals, on the other hand, do not have object identifiers. Objects and literals are characterized by their types, which define their state and behavior. State refers to the values of the properties, and behavior refers to the defined operations.

This chapter covers two languages that are part of the ODMG standard: ODL and OQL. ODL specifies a database schema over the object types allowed by the underlying object model. OQL is an ad hoc, declarative query language to retrieve data from an OODB. OQL is similar in structure to SQL, the industry-standard query language for relational databases, having the familiar select-from-where syntax. Queries are specified over a schema expressed in the ODL.

2.2   THE ODMG OBJECT DEFINITION LANGUAGE

ODL defines an object-oriented schema that is consistent with the underlying principles of the ODMG object model. Figure 2.1 provides an ODL syntax summary for the definition of a class. The class className has an extent extentName and a key keyName. The declaration of an extent for a class specifies that the database system automatically maintains a set of all instances of that class, which can be referenced by extentName. The keyName references the set of properties that can uniquely identify instances of the class. A composite key is specified by enclosing the list of properties that form the key in parentheses:

key (compositeKeypart1, compositeKeypart2)

Multiple candidate keys are separated in a list by commas:

keys key1, key2

A key declaration is optional, but a key can only be declared in the context of an extent declaration.
        The state of an object is defined by the value of its properties. The term *property* refers to either an *attribute* or a *relationship* of a class. Both attributes and relationships have a name and a type. An attribute describes a characteristic of an object itself, whereas a relationship represents a binary association between two classes. In Figure 2.1, className has an attribute attributeName of type attributeType, and a relationship relationshipName of type relationshipType. The relationshipType is either the type of the class given by the association or a collection of the associated type when the cardinality or multiplicity of the association is greater than one. In the ODMG object model, a collection can be a set, bag or list. Since the goal of an OODB system is to automatically maintain the integrity of a relationship, the declaration of a relationship includes the inverse specification for the relationship. The inverseSpecification is a scoped name, giving the name of the role of the association as a relationship in the associated class. The behavior of the class is given by the signatures of the methods defined on the class.
        Since inheritance is an important feature provided by OODBs, the ODL provides inherent support for the specification of inheritance. There are two forms of inheritance supported by ODL: inheritance of both state and behavior, and the inheritance of behavior only. A class may inherit both the state and behavior of another class as specified by the optional extends clause:

```
class subclass extends superclass
( ... )
{
    // properties and behavior specific to the subclass are defined here
};
```

```
class className
(   extent          extentName
    key             keyName )
{   attribute       attributeType attributeName;
    relationship    relationshipType relationshipName
                    inverse inverseSpecification;
    // methodSignatures;
};
```

Figure 2.1: ODL Syntax Summary

In this example, the subclass inherits both the state and behavior of the superclass, allowing for the specification of additional properties and behavior for the subclass. The ODL also provides support for the inheritance of behavior only. Since an interface describes the abstract behavior of a type, a type can inherit behavior only by using the ":" symbol, which is similar to the implements clause in Java.

```
interface interfaceName
{   // methodSignatures; };
class className: interfaceName ( ... ) { ... };
```

Both forms of inheritance can be used in combination to achieve a form of multiple inheritance:

```
class subclassName extends superclassName: interfaceName ( ... ) { ... };
```

where subclassName inherits the state and behavior of superclassName and inherits the behavior of interfaceName. Detailed examples of ODL are provided throughout the next section, which illustrates how to map object-oriented conceptual models to the ODL.

2.3   MAPPING OBJECT-ORIENTED CONCEPTUAL MODELS TO ODL

Chapter 1 provided an overview of the fundamental object database concepts using the EER and UML object-oriented conceptual models. This section uses the side-by-side illustrations from Chapter 1 to map the similar concepts from the EER and UML diagrams into an object-oriented schema expressed in the ODL. The fundamental concepts of mapping classes, attributes and associations are presented first in the context of the ABSTRACT ENTERPRISE. The mapping of class hierarchies and categories are discussed using the HOLLYWOOD ENTERPRISE as an example.

2.3.1   CLASSES, ATTRIBUTES AND ASSOCIATIONS

Recall the class A of Figure 1.3 that has simple attributes (keyOfA, attrOfA), a composite attribute (compositeOfA) and a derived attribute (derivedAttr). In ODL, class A is mapped to a class having an extent extentOfA, which uniquely identifies instances of the class using the key keyOfA. The simple attributes keyOfA and attrOfA are declared as type string, for simplicity. Since ODL provides inherent support for complex types, the composite attribute of A can be directly represented. A type CompositeStruct consisting of the composite attributes (attrA1, attrA2, and attrA3) is first defined, and the attribute compositeOfA is declared to be of type CompositeStruct. The derived attribute is defined using a get method. The signatures of the methods associated with the behavior of the class for creating new instances, destroying instances and providing standard access are also part of the class definition. For brevity, the method signatures are not included in the examples that follow.

```
struct CompositeStruct
{   string attrA1;
    string attrA2;
    string attrA3;
};
class A
(   extent extentOfA,
    key keyOfA )
{   attribute string keyOfA;
    attribute string attrOfA;
    attribute CompositeStruct compositeOfA;
    . . .
    // provide get method signature for derivedAttr
    // method signatures for behavior
};
```

The class C of Figure 1.4 illustrates a multivalued attribute, named multiValuedAttr. In the relational data model, a multivalued attribute must be mapped to its own table including the key attribute of the class. Since an object-oriented data model supports collections, multiValuedAttr can be represented directly as an attribute of C having a collection as its type. Although the set collection type is used in this example, the choice of the appropriate collection type (set, bag, or list) is ultimately based on the semantics of the enterprise.

```
class C ( . . . )
{   . . .
    attribute set<string> multiValuedAttr;
};
```

Binary associations without attributes are mapped to a relationship in the ODL. A relationship in ODL has a name, a type, and an inverse specification. As an example, consider the 1:1 bc association between the classes B and C as illustrated in Figure 1.8. In class B, define a relationship named bTOc of type C having as its inverse the relationship named cTOb in class C, which is specified as C::cTOb. In class C, the relationship cTOb is of type B with inverse B::bTOc.

```
class B (...)
{  ...
   relationship C bTOc inverse C::cTOb;
};
class C (...)
{  ...
   relationship B cTOb inverse B::bTOc;
};
```

The specification of a relationship requires the definition of its inverse since the database is responsible for maintaining the integrity of the relationship. For example, if the instance of the bTOc relationship for an object b_i is assigned the object c_j, then the database system automatically updates the instance of the relationship cTOb of c_j to the object b_i.

The cardinality ratio constraints of the association are inherent in the specification of the object-oriented schema by defining the type of the relationship and its inverse. For the bc association in Figure 1.8, the type of each association is a single object of the appropriate class. One type of constraint that is not defined implicitly in the schema is the total participation of class B in the bc association. This constraint is straightforward in the relational data model by using the not null attribute constraint. In an object-oriented database, this constraint must be handled as part of the behavior of the object. For example, the constructor method for class B must ensure that the value of the bTOc relationship is not null.

The above example illustrated the mapping to ODL for a 1:1 association. A similar template applies to a binary association without attributes having 1:N or M:N cardinality ratios. The only difference is that the type of the many side of the association is a collection. The appropriate choice for the type of the collection as set, bag or list depends on the semantics of the enterprise.

When binary associations have attributes, an association class must be introduced to represent the attributes of the association. The association class also includes two relationships - one for each class participating in the binary association. Consider the M:N ab association between classes A and B that has a descriptive attribute attrOfAB, as shown in Figure 1.6. Figure 2.2 gives the UML diagram for the corresponding reified association. An association class is defined as the class named AB, having the attribute attrOfAB and two relationships: abTOa and abTOb. The relationship abTOa is of type A, indicating the instance of class A that is participating in the relationship instance. Similarly, the relationship abTOb is of type B, indicating the instance of class B that is participating in the relationship instance. The definitions for the classes involved in the association include relationships to the new association class. Class A contains the relationship aTOab having as its type a set of AB objects, since an object of type A is related to at least one and potentially many Bs through the AB association class. Similarly, class B contains the relationship bTOab having as its type a set of AB objects, since an object of type B is related to potentially many As through the AB association class.

```
class AB
( extent extentOfAB )
```

```
{   attribute string attrOfAB;
    relationship A abTOa inverse A::aTOab;
    relationship B abTOb inverse B::bTOab;
};
class A (...)
{   ...
    relationship set<AB> aTOab inverse AB::abTOa;
};
class B (...)
{   ...
    relationship set<AB> bTOab inverse AB::abTOb;
};
```

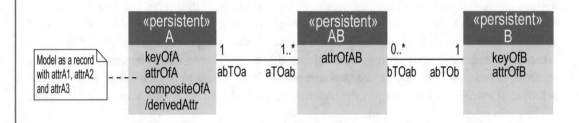

Figure 2.2: Reified M:N Association for the ABSTRACT ENTERPRISE

The mapping of recursive associations is similar to the mapping of nonrecursive associations, except that the recursive association is relating the same class to itself. In Figure 1.9, the class B has a recursive association bb. One straightforward approach to mapping a recursive association is to use the role names of the association as the name of the relationships in ODL. For example, the parent role of the bb association is of type B having the child role as its inverse relationship. The child role is a collection type, representing the children of the parent. Again, by defining a relationship, the database system is responsible for automatically maintaining the integrity of the relationship. For example, when the parent relationship instance is assigned a value, the database system automatically adds the associated object to the child relationship.

```
class B
(   extent extentOfB
    key keyOfB )
{   ...
    relationship B parent inverse B::child;
    relationship set<B> child inverse B::parent;
};
```

The mapping of N-ary associations is similar to the mapping of binary associations having descriptive attributes. An association class is defined to represent the N-ary association, and there are N relationships defined, one for each class involved in the association. Consider as an example, the ternary relationship given in Figure 1.10. In this relationship, Finance is the association class, with relationships financedBank, financedCar, and financedPerson that, respectively, refer to the Bank, Car, and Person involved in the transaction. In the inverse direction, Bank, Car, and Person define relationships that point back to Finance. The cardinality of each inverse relationship indicates the number of times an object of the class can participate in a Finance association. The relationships in Bank and Person, for example, are set-valued, indicating that a bank can finance may cars and a person can buy many cars. The relationship in Car is single-valued, indicating that a car can only be sold once to a person.

```
class Finance
(   extent extentOfFinance )
{   attribute real loanAmount;
    relationship Bank financedBank inverse Bank::carsFinanced;
    relationship Car financedCar inverse Car::financedBy;
    relationship Person financedPerson inverse Person::carsFinanced;
};
class Bank (...)
{   ...
    relationship set<Finance> carsFinanced inverse Finance::financedBank;
};
class Car (...)
{   ...
    relationship Finance financedBy inverse Finance::financedCar;
};
class Person (...)
{   ...
    relationship set<Finance> carsFinanced inverse Finance::financedPerson;
};
```

The UML conceptual class diagrams have the ability to represent unidirectional associations through navigability. Unidirectional associations store the association in one direction. Since a relationship in ODL requires an inverse specification, relationships are inherently bidirectional. To define a unidirectional association in ODL, use an attribute whose value is a class type. For example, the unidirectional bc association shown in Figure 1.12 is defined as an attribute in class B having the type C. It is possible to derive the inverse direction of the unidirectional association by providing a method in C to derive the B values to which it is related.

```
class B ( ... )
{  ...
   attribute C bc;
};
```

A weak class in an EER diagram is typically related to its identifying owner by a 1:N relationship. In Figure 1.13, the Weak class is related to its identifying owner class A by its identifying
relationship dependsOn. The candidate key of a weak class is formed by the combination of the
primary key of its identifying owner and its own partial key, which uniquely identifies the weak object
in the context of the identifying owner. In the UML diagram of Figure 1.13, dependsOn represents
a qualified association based on the partialKey. One way to map this type of an association is to
define a relationship that links the weak class to its identifying owner. For the semantics expressed in
Figure 1.13, the relationship linkToWeak defined in class A represents the collection of Weak objects
associated with an instance of class A. The inverse relationship defined as linkToOwner in the Weak
class links the Weak instance to its identifying owner instance, which is of type A having the attribute
keyOfA as its candidate key. One may also choose to maintain the extent of the Weak class, which
requires storing the value of the key of the identifying owner (keyOfA) to use in combination with
the partialKey.

```
class A
(  extent extentOfA
   key keyOfA )
{  attribute string keyOfA;
   relationship set<Weak> linkToWeak inverse Weak::linkToOwner;
   ...
};
class Weak
(  extent extentOfWeak
   key (keyOfA, partialKey) )
{  attribute string partialKey;
   attribute string keyOfA;
   relationship A linkToOwner inverse A::linkToWeak;
   ...
};
```

2.3.1.1 Constraints on Classes, Attributes and Associations

When mapping the object-oriented conceptual data models to an object-oriented data model, there
are a number of constraints that need to be captured at the implementation level. These constraints
on classes, attributes, and associations include the specification of candidate keys, referential integrity,
as well as participation and multiplicity constraints.

In ODL, there is a key clause to specify the uniqueness of candidate keys, and referential
integrity is inherent in the specification of the type of a property. The type specification in ODL

also inherently supports a simple cardinality constraint. For example, the type of a property is a class type when the property is related to one object of that type or a collection of a class type when the property is related to more than one object of that type.

For more complicated participation and multiplicity constraints, the constraints must be implemented as part of the behavior of the object. A total participation constraint requires that the behavior for constructing an object and modifying the property verify that the value of the property is not null. This verification is written in the underlying OOPL for the OODB. Similarly, verifying specific multiplicity constraints (other than the simple one-to-one or one-to-many cardinality constraints that are inherent in the specification of relationships) requires the constraint to be checked in the behavior of the object.

2.3.1.2 Checkpoint: ODL Mapping of Classes, Attributes and Associations

Table 2.1 summarizes the mapping of classes, attributes, and associations to ODL, using the names C, C1 and C2 to represent generic classes. In the table, the first column indicates the component being mapped to the object model. The second column provides the name of the class to which the ODL definition is added. The third column indicates the required definition in ODL to realize the component in the object model. As indicated in the table, ODL inherently supports the specification of class, attributes, and associations. The specification of class hierarchies in ODL is described in the next section.

Table 2.1: Summary of ODL Mapping Heuristics for Classes, Attributes, and Associations.

Component	Class	ODL Definition
class C	C	class C (extent extentOfC)
single-valued or composite attribute s of C	C	attribute typeOfS s;
multivalued attribute m of C	C	attribute set < typeOfElementInM > m;
binary association – no attributes (1:1 shown)	C1 C2	relationship C2 c1TOc2 inverse C2::c2TOc1; relationship C1 c2TOc1 inverse C1::c1TOc2;

binary association ac with attributes (e.g., attrOfAC) Use an association class (M:N shown)	C1
	
	C2
	
	AC
		relationship set < AC > c1TOac
		    inverse AC::acTOc1;
		relationship set < AC > c2TOac
		    inverse AC::acTOc2;
		attribute typeOfAttrOfAC attrOfAC;
		relationship C1 acTOc1 inverse C1::c1TOac;
		relationship C2 acTOc2 inverse C2::c2TOac;

recursive association cc (1:N shown)	C	relationship C parent inverse C::child; relationship set < C > child inverse C::parent;

2.3.2   CLASS HIERARCHIES

Object-oriented schemas provide inherent support for the specification of class hierarchies. In ODL, the inheritance of state and behavior is supported by the **extends** clause. Consider as an example the **Person** class hierarchy from the HOLLYWOOD ENTERPRISE, which represents a partial specialization of **Person** into its disjoint subclasses **MovieProfessional** and **Celebrity**.

```
class Person
( ... )
{ ... };
class MovieProfessional extends Person
( ... )
{
    // Specific properties and methods for MovieProfessional
};
class Celebrity extends Person
( ... )
{
    // Specific properties and methods for Celebrity
};
```

The EER and UML conceptual data models both provide support for the specification of specialization constraints: disjoint versus overlapping specialization, and total or mandatory participation in the class specialization. An OODB uses its underlying OOPL as the basis of its semantics for specialization constraints. Most OOPLs do not provide for an overlapping specialization of subclasses. Therefore, by default, a specialization in an OODB is disjoint. If an overlapping specialization is required for the application, then the programmer can be creative to simulate the inheritance by using an explicit reference to the superclass and calling its methods. The total specialization constraint is also based on the semantics of the underlying OOPL. For a total specialization, the superclass can be specified as an abstract class if permitted by the programming language. Otherwise, the total specialization constraint must be built-in to the behavior of the objects.

For the mapping of shared subclasses, most OOPLs do not directly support multiple inheritance of both state and behavior. ODL does not support the specification of shared subclasses. Multiple inheritance can be simulated in a class definition by using the extends clause to inherit state and behavior from one class and by using the interface feature to inherit only behavior from another class. This is a common programming practice in OOPLs.

2.3.3   CATEGORIES

A category in the EER or the Xor constraint in UML can be represented by introducing a class for the category. Properties are introduced in the category class to represent the association to its related superclasses. Consider as an example the partial **Sponsor** category from the HOLLYWOOD ENTER-

PRISE where a Sponsor is either a Person or a Company. A unidirectional association, modeled as an attribute in ODL, is added to the category class for each class participating in the category. The Sponsor class has two attributes: personSponsor and companySponsor. Only one of the unidirectional attributes can have a value, indicating the type of the Sponsor category as either a Person or a Company. The other unidirectional attribute must always be null since a Sponsor cannot be both a Person and a Company. This category constraint must be implemented within the behavior of the (Sponsor) category class.

```
class Person
(   extent persons
    key ... )
{   ... };
class Company
(   extent companies
    key ... )
{ ... };
class Sponsor
(   extent sponsors )
{   attribute Person personSponsor;
    attribute Company companySponsor;

    ...
};
```

When the category is partial, the unidirectional association is preferable. It is still possible to find out whether a person or company is a sponsor and the projects that they sponsor by navigating the unidirectional associations from the Sponsor class. If the category is total, requiring that each superclass participates in the category, then the category associations can be implemented using bidirectional relationships. The relationship provides an explicit access path to the category class. The behavior of the superclasses must enforce the total categorization constraint by verifying that the relationship value to the category class is not null. Again, the category class must enforce the exclusive-or constraint of the category.

2.3.4   CHECKPOINT: MAPPING TO ODL

An object-oriented database schema provides inherent support for most of the constraints specified in the object-oriented conceptual data models. The constraints that are not captured in ODL must be implemented as part of the behavior of the object. Figure 2.3 gives the ODL mapping of the HOLLYWOOD ENTERPRISE. Figure 2.4 provides the UML diagram that corresponds to the ODL specification. Since ODL does not inherently support overlapping subclasses, the specialization of Celebrity into the MovieStar and Model subclasses are now disjoint. The Paid association class of Figure 2.4 is represented as a reified association, which corresponds to its ODL specification. Since the Sponsor category is not total, the associations relating a Sponsor to its corresponding superclass are unidirectional.

2.4   THE ODMG OBJECT QUERY LANGUAGE

OQL is based on the SQL industry-standard query language for relational databases. In SQL, the basic select-from-where clause selects a list of attributes from the specified tables where a condition holds. The from clause specifies the tables that are relevant to answering the query, allowing for table aliases or variables to range over tuples of a table. The where clause describes the conditions that must hold on the data in the tables to be selected as a result of the query. The select clause gives a list of attributes from the relevant tables that are to appear in the query result.

OQL also has the familiar format of the select-from-where clause. Since OQL is based on an object model, the from clause specifies the collections of objects that are relevant to answering the query and uses variables to range over the relevant object collections. Recall that the ODL provides for the definition of an extent, and the name of an extent denotes a collection of objects of the same type. Variables in the from clause typically range over extents or the multivalued properties of an object. The where clause similarly describes the properties that must hold for the data to be in the result of the query. The select clause in OQL also defines the structure of the result of the query, but OQL's select clause is more expressive than its relational counterpart, which will be illustrated through examples later in this chapter.

To summarize, an OQL query has the following format:

select   *defines the data to be returned and its structure*
from   *specifies collections relevant to answering the query and*
          identifiers to iterate over those collections
where   *specifies conditions for filtering objects*

Consider a simple query over the HOLLYWOOD schema given in Figure 2.3 that finds the titles of the movies filmed in "Phoenix":

select   f.title
from   f in filmProjects
where   f.location = "Phoenix";

The properties of an object are accessed using the familiar dot notation from object-oriented programming languages. In the from clause, the variable identifier f ranges over the objects in the filmProjects extent. The where clause finds the filmProject objects having a location value of "Phoenix". The select clause returns the title of the selected film projects. Note that the from clause could have used the SQL-like syntax where the identifier appears after the expression over which the variable ranges, e.g., filmProjects f. The exposition in this book follows the syntactical convention of identifier in expression.

```
class Person
( extent people
  key pId )
{ attribute string pId;
  attribute string name;
  attribute string gender;
  attribute string phone;
  attribute string address;
  attribute Person isMarriedTo; ...
};
class MovieProfessional extends Person
( extent movieProfessionals)
{ attribute string company; ...
}
class Celebrity extends Person
( extent celebrities )
{ attribute date birthDate;
  relationship Agent celebrityAgent inverse Agent::agentFor; ...
};
class MovieStar extends Celebrity
( extent movieStars )
{ attribute string movieType;
  relationship set<FilmProject> actsIn inverse FilmProject::actors; ...
};
class Model extends Celebrity
( extent models )
{ attribute string preferences;
  relationship set<Paid> modelsInProjects inverse Paid::modelOfProject; ...
};
class Critic extends MovieProfessional
( extent critics )
{ attribute string popularity; ...
};
class Agent extends MovieProfessional
( extent agents )
{ attribute float agentFee;
  relationship set<Celebrity> agentFor inverse Celebrity::celebrityAgent; ...
};
```

Figure 2.3: ODL Schema for the Hollywood Enterprise *(Continues.)*

```
class Project
( extent projects
  key projectId )
{ attribute string projectId;
  attribute string location;
  attribute float cost;
  attribute string type; ...
};
class FilmProject extends Project
( extent filmProjects )
{ attribute string title;
  relationship set<MovieStar> actors inverse MovieStar::actsIn; ...
};
class ModelingProject extends Project
( extent modelingProjects )
{ attribute string description;
  relationship set<Paid> paidModels
            inverse Paid::paidByProject;
  relationship Sponsor sponsoredBy inverse Sponsor::projectsSponsored; ...
};
class Paid
( extent paidModelsInProjects )
{ attribute float salary;
  relationship Model modelOfProject inverse Model::modelsInProjects;
  relationship ModelingProject paidByProject inverse ModelingProject::paidModels; ...
};
class Company
( extent companies
  key cId )
{ attribute string cId;
  attribute string cName; ...
};
class Sponsor
( extent sponsors )
{ attribute Person personSponsor;
  attribute Company companySponsor;
  relationship set<ModelingProject> projectsSponsored
            inverse ModelingProject::sponsoredBy; ...
};
```

Figure 2.3: *(Continued.)* ODL Schema for the Hollywood Enterprise

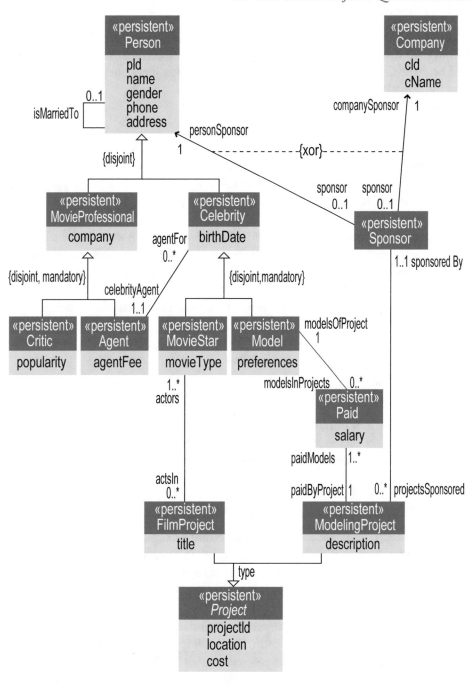

Figure 2.4: UML Diagram for the ODL Specification of the HOLLYWOOD ENTERPRISE

2.4.1   PATH EXPRESSIONS

Path expressions allow navigation from one object to another. OQL uses either the dot (.) notation or the arrow (→) notation to indicate a path expression. For example, assume that the variable c is defined over the Celebrity class. The following path expressions return the name of the agent's spouse for the celebrity given by c:

- c.celebrityAgent.isMarriedTo.name

- c→celebrityAgent→isMarriedTo→name

The property celebrityAgent denotes the Agent of the celebrity. Since an Agent is a Person, the isMarriedTo property denotes the Person married to the agent. The name property gives the name of the spouse. Rather than using multiple notations, this book follows the convention of using dot notation for path expressions.

In the preceding example, the properties in the path expressions were single-valued attributes. OQL does not allow path expressions to traverse over multivalued attributes and relationships. The query must be expressed so that all variables over multivalued properties are explicitly defined in the from clause.

Consider as an example a query to retrieve the names of movie stars that appear in film projects located in "Phoenix":

```
select    a.name
from      f in filmProjects,
          a in f.actors
where     f.location = "Phoenix";
```

The variable identifier a is introduced in the from clause to range over the actors multivalued property of a filmProject that is located in "Phoenix". The actors property is a set of MovieStar objects that act in the film project. Since a MovieStar is a Person, the select clause returns the name of the actor.

2.4.2   OQL EXPRESSIONS AND QUERY RESULTS

In the examples of OQL presented so far, the select clause looks quite similar to that of SQL. Query results in SQL are a collection of tuples or structures that are formed by listing the desired attributes. If the keyword distinct is used, the collection is a *set* of tuples. Otherwise, the collection is a *multiset* or *bag* of tuples, allowing duplicate elements. However, the results of query expressions in OQL are more expressive than in SQL.

Expressions in OQL yield atoms, structures, collections, and literals as results. The type of a result can be inferred from the query expression. The result type of the previous example that retrieves the names of movie stars appearing in film projects located in "Phoenix" is *bag* < *string* >.

The select clause in OQL can return a collection of structured results. Consider the query that retrieves the name of the actor and the actor's agent for each actor in the film project named "Days of Thunder":

```
select      struct( movieStarName: a.name,
                         agentName: a.celebrityAgent.name )
from        f in filmProjects, a in f.actors
where       f.title = "Days of Thunder";
```

For each field of the structure, the label is specified along with the source of the field. In this case, the label for the name of the movie star is movieStarName, and the label for the name of the actor's agent is agentName. The result type of the query is

$$bag < struct(movieStarName : string, agentName : string) >.$$

Consider another query that returns a collection of sponsor objects along with the set of the sponsored modeling projects:

```
select      struct( sponsorObject: s, projectsOf: s.projectsSponsored )
from        s in sponsors;
```

The result type of the query is

$$bag < struct(sponsorObject : Sponsor, projectsOf : set < ModelingProject >) >.$$

Queries do not always have to use the select-from-where clause. A database extent (e.g., filmProjects) is a valid OQL query expression. Other examples of valid OQL queries that do not use the select-from-where syntax include path expressions involving a named persistent object as a database entry point.

2.4.2.1 Define Statement
The define statement gives a persistent name to a query expression. The define statement is similar to a view in SQL. For example, the object phxFilms is defined as the collection of film projects located in "Phoenix":

```
define      phxFilms as
select      f
from        f in filmProjects
where       f.location = "Phoenix";
```

Although this query is similar to the query that returned the titles of the film projects located in "Phoenix", this query returns the corresponding FilmProject objects. The type of phxFilms is $bag < FilmProject >$.

The define statement can also be used to identify a named persistent object. In the following example, the name daysOfThunder is defined as the film project whose title is "Days of Thunder". The subquery returns a bag of FilmProject objects. The element operator returns a singleton of type FilmProject. Note that an error results if there is more than one object in the operand to the element operator. In this case, an error occurs if there is more than one film project having the name "Days of Thunder".

```
define     daysOfThunder as
element   ( select          f
           from            f in filmProjects
           where           f.title = "Days of Thunder" );
```

Defined expressions can then be used to return other values. For example, daysOfThunder.cost is a valid OQL query expression.

2.4.2.2 Methods in Queries

OQL allows methods to be used in queries in the same way as attributes. As an example, assume that the Celebrity class has an age method that calculates the age of a celebrity using birthDate. The following query finds the names of celebrities under the age of 30:

```
select     c.name
from       c in celebrities
where      c.age < 30;
```

The query result type is $bag < string >$.

2.4.2.3 Embedded Queries

OQL is a well-typed language. Queries can be embedded in the select and from clauses provided that the type system is respected. Consider an example that embeds a query in the from clause where the variable phx iterates over the embedded query that returns the FilmProject objects located in "Phoenix":

```
select     struct(title: phx.title, cost: phx.cost )
from       phx in  ( select f
                     from f in filmProjects
                     where f.location = "Phoenix" )
where      phx.cost > 10,000,000;
```

This query retrieves the title and cost of film projects located in "Phoenix" that cost more than 10 million. The query result type is $bag < struct(title : string, cost : float) >$.

Queries can also be embedded in the select clause. Consider a query that returns the names of the celebrities that an agent manages:

```
select     struct( agentName: a.name,
                   agentForCelebrities: (select c.name from c in a.agentFor))
from       a in agents;
```

This query returns the name of each agent and the names of celebrities managed by that agent. The query result type is

$$bag < struct(agentName :string, agentForCelebrities :bag < string >) >.$$

2.4.3   SET MEMBERSHIP AND QUANTIFICATION

OQL also supports queries involving set membership as well as existential and universal quantification. The type of these queries is a Boolean value: TRUE or FALSE.

Queries testing membership in a set use the syntax

e in c

returning TRUE if the element e is in the collection c. Consider as an example the query that determines whether daysOfThunder is in phxFilms:

daysOfThunder in phxFilms;

OQL allows for queries involving quantification, both existential and universal. The syntax for existential quantification is

exists i in c: exp

returning TRUE if at least one element of the collection c satisfies the exp expression, where the variable i iterates over elements in the collection. For example, the following query determines whether there any film projects located in "Phoenix":

exists f in filmProjects: f.location = "Phoenix";

Consider a more complicated query that identifies those models that have at least one modeling project located in "Phoenix".

```
select    modelName: m.name
from      m in models
where     exists p in m.modelsInProjects:
          p.paidByProject.location = "Phoenix";
```

The query returns the name of a model if there exists a modeling project for that model that is located in "Phoenix".

The syntax for universal quantification is

for all i in c: exp

returning TRUE if all elements in the collection c satisfy the exp expression. As an example, the following query tests whether all film projects cost more than $10 million.

for all f in filmProjects: f.cost > 10,000,000;

The query below lists the movie stars for which all of their film projects cost more than $20 million, illustrating the use of the universal quantifier in the where clause of a query.

```
select    m.name
from      m in movieStars
where     for all fp in m.actsIn: fp.cost > 20,000,000;
```

As a more complex example, consider a query that uses both existential and universal quantification to find the name of the companies for which all of their sponsored modeling projects include at least one male model:

```
select    s.companySponsor.cName
from      s in sponsors
where     s.companySponsor <> null and
          for all mp in s.projectsSponsored:
          (exists p in mp.paidModels: p.modelOfProject.gender = "M");
```

2.4.4   ORDERING

OQL provides the familiar order by clause with the keywords asc and desc used to specify ascending or descending order, respectively. The following query provides a list in descending order of the costs of film projects located in "Phoenix" along with the title of the film:

```
select    struct(phxTitle: fp.title, phxCost: fp.cost)
from      fp in filmProjects
where     fp.location = "Phoenix"
order by  fp.cost desc;
```

When ordering is used, the collection is considered a list, which is a sequenced collection. The result type of the example query is $list < struct(phxTitle : string, phxCost : float) >$.

The order by clause can also be used in embedded queries to generate a list. The query below provides an alphabetical order of movie stars for each film project filmed in "Phoenix":

```
select    struct( phxTitle: fp.title,
                  phxMovieStars:   ( select ms.name
                                     from ms in fp.actors
                                     order by ms.name ))
from      fp in filmProjects
where     fp.location = "Phoenix"
order by  fp.title asc;
```

The query result type is

$$list < struct(phxTitle : string, phxMovieStars : list < string >) >.$$

2.4.5   USING COLLECTIONS

Collections are an important feature of OODBs. OQL provides explicit operators for extracting elements from a collection and for manipulating collections. Earlier in the chapter when defining the persistent named object daysOfThunder, the element operator illustrated the extraction of an element from a collection that consisted of a singleton. A singleton collection is common when the query is selecting an object based on the value of the key. Note that an error results if there is more than one object in the operand to the element operator.

OQL also provides explicit notation for extracting the first, last, and indexed elements from an indexed collection, such as a list. For example, by ordering a collection of model name and salary pairs for modeling projects located in Phoenix in ascending order on salary, the last operator returns the model and salary for the highest paid model. This query assumes that there is only one model having the highest salary.

```
last (select    struct(modelName: m.name, modelSalary: p.salary)
      from      m in models, p in m.modelsInProjects
      where     p.paidByProject.located = "Phoenix"
      order by  modelSalary asc) ;
```

By reordering the query in descending order on salary, an indexed expression returns the top ten paid models for a Phoenix modeling project. Note that the index of the first element is 0 so the indexed expression [0:9] returns the first 10 elements.

```
( select    struct(modelName: m.name, modelSalary: p.salary)
  from      m in models, p in m.modelsInProjects
  where     p.paidByProject.location = "Phoenix"
  order by modelSalary desc) [0:9];
```

The result type of the query is

$$list < struct(modelName : string, modelSalary : float) >.$$

2.4.6   AGGREGATION AND GROUPING

OQL provides aggregate operators (min, max, count, sum, avg) over a collection of the appropriate type. The operators min, max, sum, and avg must have an operand collection of numerical elements, where count counts the number of elements of any type in the operand collection. As an example of count, find the number of film projects in which a movie star has acted:

```
select    struct ( name: m.name,
                   filmCount: count(m.actsIn) )
from      m in movieStars
order by  name asc;
```

The property actsIn for a MovieStar is a collection, in this case a set, of FilmProject objects in which the movie star has acted.

The following query finds the total salary of a model for all of the modeling projects in which they model:

```
select    struct ( name: m.name,
                   salaryTotal: sum(select p.salary from p in m.modelsInProjects) )
from      m in models
order by  name asc;
```

Since OQL is well-typed, the use of aggregation over a collection is more intuitive than aggregation in SQL, which requires understanding the implicit operation of the aggregation in conjunction with the group by clause. SQL also requires that any non-aggregate attribute in the select clause appear in the group by clause. The group by clause in OQL, although similar to the corresponding clause in SQL, provides an explicit reference to the collection of objects within each group or partition.

The result type of a grouping specification is always of the type

$$set < struct(grouping Fields, partition : bag < struct(fromIterators) >) >$$

where

- groupingFields consists of the fields and their types in the group by clause,

- partition is a distinguished field representing the result of the grouping, and

- fromIterators consists of the variables and their types used in the from clause to iterate over collections.

Consider the following query that returns a count and a set of the models that an agent represents by grouping the models based on the name of the model's agent:

```
select      struct( agentName: m.celebrityAgent.name,
                    modelCount: count(partition),
                    modelNames: (select p.m.name from p in partition))
from        m in models
group by agentName: m.celebrityAgent.name;
```

The result type of the grouping specification is

$$set < struct(agentName : string, partition : bag < struct(m : Model) >) >$$

For each group given by the agentName, there is a distinguished field called partition that gives the values of the iterator variables used in the from clause using a structure. To find the number of models that the agent represents, the aggregate operator count counts the number of models in the partition. To retrieve the names of the models from the group, the select clause uses an embedded query to iterate over the elements in the partition. Since the partition always returns a structure consisting of the variables in the from clause, dot notation (p.m.name) is used to access a field from within the group. The result type of a group by query is always a set since there is exactly one partition for each value of the grouping fields. The result type of the example query is

$$set < struct(agentName : string, modelCount : integer, modelNames : bag < string >) >$$

Just as in SQL, a having clause filters the partitioned sets. To return only the agents that represent more than 3 models, append the following having clause to the prior query specification:

$$having\ count(partition) > 3$$

2.4.7   CHECKPOINT: OQL

Although OQL looks similar to the SQL industry standard, it is important to think out of the relational box when answering queries in OQL. Consider the query to retrieve the name and preferences of models who work on modeling projects located in "Phoenix". As in SQL, there are several ways to correctly answer this query in OQL. One solution is to start from the models extent and determine whether the model models in projects that are located in "Phoenix":

```
select      struct( modelName: m.name,
                    modelPreferences: m.preferences )
from        m in models, p in m.modelsInProjects
where       p.paidByProject.location = "Phoenix";
```

Another solution is to start from modeling projects that are located in "Phoenix" and find the corresponding models:

```
select      struct( modelName: p.modelOfProject.name,
                    modelPreferences: p.modelOfProject.preferences )
from        mp in modelingProjects, p in mp.paidModels
where       mp.location = "Phoenix";
```

Both of these solutions represented an object-oriented approach that navigates through the associations between objects.

2.5   CASE STUDY: LINQ AND DB4O

The OQL of the ODMG contributes a test bed for the study of query optimization techniques for object databases and a database independent way to describe declarative queries over the ODMG object model. Although the OQL standard was only implemented in research prototypes rather than commercial OODBs, it provides an important foundation for declarative querying capabilities over objects. There are more similarities than differences between OQL and the recently introduced Language INtegrated Query (LINQ) language embedded into the OOPLs of the .NET Framework. Both languages rely on the well-typed features of the underlying OOPL, e.g., applying aggregate operators to a collection of the appropriate type. LINQ is a declarative query language that is seamlessly integrated into the OOPLs of the .NET Framework, which include C# and Visual Basic. LINQ can query collections of objects, tuples, or XML elements. In this case study, the focus is on querying a collection of objects using the C# language. Therefore, the fields of the classes are implemented as properties in C#, which are conventionally indicated by a method with an initial uppercase letter that defines get and set accessors for the private instance field that the property is encapsulating. The private instance field usually has the same name but starts with an initial lowercase letter. The case study concludes with an overview of the db4o open-source OODB and the use of LINQ for db4o native queries in C#.

2.5.1   LINQ

LINQ builds on the familiarity of SQL and OQL with from-where-select clauses that follow the underlying execution order of the query:

from   *specifies collections relevant to answering the query and*
        identifiers to iterate over those collections
where   *specifies conditions for filtering objects*
select *defines the structure of the data to be returned*

LINQ also uses the familiar path expressions with dot notation to access properties or methods associated with objects. The query to find the titles of the movies filmed in "Phoenix" in LINQ is:

```
from    f in filmProjects
where   f.Location == "Phoenix"
select  f.Title;
```

Note that the from and where clauses in LINQ are not limited to occur once in the expression, and the clauses can be intertwined, as in the following query to find the actors who starred in projects filmed in "Phoenix":

```
from    f in filmProjects
where   f.Location == "Phoenix"
from    a in f.Actors
select  a.Name;
```

LINQ's querying capabilities are provided by the underlying .NET framework, which includes *extension methods*. An extension method is a static method in a static class that can be invoked as if it were an instance method on the object itself. The familiar from-where-select syntax in LINQ, which is called *query comprehension syntax*, is compiled into an *extension method syntax*. For example, Where and Select are extension methods. Therefore, the underlying extension method syntax for the query returning titles of movies filmed in "Phoenix" is the following:

```
filmProjects.Where(f => f.Location == "Phoenix").Select(f => f.Title);
```

The Where extension method is invoked on the filmProjects extent, taking as an argument an anonymous function that filters the extent. The => syntax is read as "*goes to*" and represents a way to pass an argument into an anonymous function similar to lambda expressions. The Select method returns the Title of the filtered collection.

The collection of extension methods that perform operations on LINQ query expressions are called *query operators*. As will be shown in the following examples, queries typically use a combination of query comprehension syntax with query operators.

2.5.1.1 Query Results

An important feature of the underlying framework used by LINQ is implicitly typed variables. The keyword var defines a variable with an implicit type. Consider defining the variable phxFilms as the collection of film projects located in "Phoenix":

```
var phxFilms =
      from      f in filmProjects
      where     f.Location == "Phoenix"
      select    f;
```

In C#, the type of the collection returned is usually an instance of IEnumerable<T>. This exposition will continue to use the generic term *collection* rather than emphasize the C# type system, which is not required to understand the fundamentals of LINQ. This is consistent with the earlier discussion of OQL, in which the particular language binding was not discussed. The type of the collections were described using the terms *bag* and *set*. Recall that a *bag* is a collection that may contain duplicate elements, and a *set* is a collection that does not contain duplicate elements. To remove duplicate elements from a collection in LINQ, the Distinct operator is used. For example, the following query returns the *set* of movie stars that appeared in Phoenix film projects:

```
( from      f in phxFilms
  from      a in f.Actors
  select    a).Distinct();
```

In addition to collections, LINQ can return a single object, with its type being implicitly defined. Consider defining a variable daysOfThunder that represents the unique FilmProject object with the title "Days of Thunder":

```
var daysOfThunder =
    ( from      f in filmProjects
      where     f.Title == "Days of Thunder"
      select    f).Single();
```

This query illustrates the use of the Single operator that returns the single object from a collection, throwing an exception if there is more than one object in the collection to which it is applied.

LINQ query expressions return structured results using the features of anonymous types and object initialization. The following query returns an anonymous type that contains the names of movie stars in the daysOfThunder film along with the name of each movie star's agent:

```
from      a in daysOfThunder.Actors
select    new { movieStarName = a.Name,
                agentName = a.CelebrityAgent.Name };
```

The anonymous type feature is illustrated by the new operator in the select clause, creating an anonymous type. The braces enclose the initialization of the anonymous object using names, which is in contrast to conventional constructors for named classes that use the position of the parameter in the call to the constructor for initialization.

Queries can use method calls as shown in the following query that finds celebrities who are younger than 30:

```
from      c in celebrities
where     c.Age() < 30
select    c.Name;
```

LINQ also supports embedded queries in the from or select clauses. Consider as an example a query embedded in the from clause to find the "Phoenix" film projects, which is then filtered for a cost greater than $10 million:

```
from      phx in  ( from f in filmProjects
                        where f.Location == "Phoenix"
                        select f)
where     phx.Cost > 10,000,000
select    new {   phx.Title, phx.Cost };
```

Queries can also be embedded in the select clause. This query returns the names of the celebrities that an agent manages:

```
from      a in agents
select    new { agentName = a.Name,
                    agentForCelebrities = (from c in a.AgentFor select c.Name) };
```

2.5.1.2 Set Membership and Quantification

LINQ also supports set membership and quantification queries using query operators, such as Contains, Any, and All.

The following query returns a Boolean result of TRUE if the collection phxFilms contains the film project daysOfThunder, using the Contains operator on phxFilms with daysOfThunder as a parameter:

```
phxFilms.Contains(daysOfThunder);
```

The Any operator supports existential quantification. In the following example, an anonymous function is a parameter to the Any operator, returning TRUE if there is any f in filmProjects having a Location value equal to "Phoenix":

```
filmProjects.Any(f => f.Location == "Phoenix");
```

As a more complicated example, consider the query that finds the models who have had at least one modeling project located in "Phoenix":

```
from      m in models
where     (m.ModelsInProjects).Any(p => p.PaidByProject.Location == "Phoenix")
select    new {modelname = m.Name};
```

The All operator supports universal quantification. In this simple example, an anonymous function determines whether all f objects in filmProjects cost more than 10 million:

```
filmProjects.All(f => f.Cost > 10000000);
```

Consider another query that illustrates the use of the All operator, finding the names of movie stars for which all of their film projects cost more than $20 million:

```
from      m in movieStars
where     (m.ActsIn).All(fp => fp.Cost > 20000000)
select    m.Name;
```

As a more complicated example, the following query combines universal and existential quantification by finding the sponsors that are companies for which all of their sponsored modeling projects include at least one male model:

```
from      s in sponsors
where     s.CompanySponsor ! = null &&
          (s.ProjectsSponsored).All(mp =>
               (mp.PaidModels).Any(p => p.ModelOfProject.Gender == "M"))
select    s.CompanySponsor.CName;
```

2.5.1.3 Ordering

Another common construct in a query language is the capability to order results. In LINQ, orderby is one word, and the keywords ascending and descending specify the result order, with ascending as the default. The orderby clause occurs before the select clause, allowing the results to be ordered by data that is not contained in the query result. The following query provides a list of film projects filmed in "Phoenix" sorted in descending order by the cost of the project.

```
from      fp in filmProjects
where     fp.Location == "Phoenix"
orderby   fp.Cost descending
select    new { phxTitle = fp.Title, phxCost = fp.Cost};
```

The orderby clause can also be used in embedded queries. The query below returns a list of movie stars in alphabetical order for each film project filmed in "Phoenix":

```
from      fp in filmProjects
where     fp.Location == "Phoenix"
orderby   fp.Title ascending
select    new { phxTitle = fp.Title,
               phxMovieStars = ( from ms in fp.Actors  .
                                orderby ms.Name
                                select ms.Name ) };
```

2.5.1.4 Using Collections

There are various query operators that are available in LINQ for accessing elements in a collection, such as First, Last, and Take. For example, the following query finds the highest paid Phoenix model by ordering the collection results in ascending order by salary and choosing the last element in the collection using the Last operator:

```
( from     m in models
  from     p in m.ModelsInProjects
  where    p.PaidByProject.Location == "Phoenix"
  orderby  p.Salary ascending
  select   new {modelName = m.Name, modelSalary = p.Salary}).Last();
```

As another example, consider a query that finds the top ten models based on the salary received for a modeling project in Phoenix sorted in descending order using the Take operator to return the first ten results:

```
( from     m in models
  from     p in m.ModelsInProjects
  where    p.PaidByProject.Location == "Phoenix"
  orderby  p.Salary descending
  select   new {modelName = m.Name, modelSalary = p.Salary}).Take(10);
```

Additional query operators for collections include the set operations of union (Union), intersection (Intersect), and difference (Except). There are also query operators to perform aggregation over collections.

2.5.1.5 Aggregation and Grouping

Aggregation in LINQ is a straightforward application of the appropriate operator on the desired collection. For example, the Count operator on the ActsIn property of a movie star determines the number of films for that movie star:

```
from     m in movieStars
orderby  m.Name
select   new {name = m.Name, filmCount = m.ActsIn.Count()};
```

When using the other aggregate query operators on a collection of numeric elements, such as Sum, Min, Max, and Average, the operator is applied to an appropriately type collection. For example, to find the total salary for a model requires summing the salary from all of the modeling projects for that model:

```
from     m in models
select   new { name = m.Name,
               salaryTotal =   ( from p in m.ModelsInProjects
                                 select p.Salary ).Sum()};
```

The subquery (from p in m.ModelsInProjects select p.Salary) returns a collection of the salary for that model, on which the Sum operator operates.

There is an alternative to creating the explicit collection of numbers. An anonymous function can be used to generate the numeric collection as an argument to the operator. For example, the total cost of Phoenix film projects can be found using the following query expression:

```
phxFilms.Sum(phx => phx.Cost);
```

Another useful feature of LINQ query expressions is the ability to order the query results based on the aggregation. LINQ supports a let clause to define a variable for the scope of the query. Consider ordering the results of the total model salary in descending order based on the computed salary:

```
from      m in models
let       salaryTotal = m.ModelsInProjects.Sum(p => p.Salary)
orderby   salaryTotal descending
select    new { name = m.Name,
                salaryTotal };
```

Grouping in LINQ is very different from SQL. Grouping is specified explicitly using a group clause that specifies *what to group* and *what to group by*, returning a collection of groups where each group has a Key property consisting of the value on which the group was created.

Consider a sample query that groups film projects by their location:

```
var filmsByLocation =
    from      f in filmProjects
    group     f by f.Location;
```

Subsequent queries can iterate over this collection of groups, as in the following example that returns the location, a count of the number of films associated with that location, and the group of films.

```
from      locFilms in filmsByLocation
orderby   locFilms.Key
select    new { location = locFilms.Key,
                numberOfFilms = locFilms.Count(),
                films = locFilms };
```

Alternatively, LINQ's group clause provides an optional into specification to automatically continue the iteration over the groups in one query expression.

```
from      f in filmProjects
group     f by f.Location into locFilms
orderby   locFilms.Key
select    new { location = locFilms.Key,
                numberOfFilms = locFilms.Count(),
                films = locFilms };
```

As another example, consider grouping models by their agent, returning for each agent that represents more than three models, the count and names of the models in the group.

```
from      m in models
group     m by m.CelebrityAgent into agentGroup
where     agentGroup.Count() > 3
select    new { agentName = agentGroup.Key.Name,
                modelCount = agentGroup.Count(),
                modelNames = (from mg in agentGroup select mg.Name) };
```

Note that the filtering of a group is accomplished in LINQ by a where clause following the group-by-into clause, rather than a having clause as in SQL.

2.5.1.6 Query Execution

As discussed earlier, LINQ's query comprehension syntax is converted to an underlying extension method syntax, resulting in an expression tree that represents the definition of the query. In general, a LINQ query is not executed until it is referenced, decoupling the query construction from its execution. This feature is known as *deferred query execution*. Thus, a LINQ query is similar to a database view definition in that it is materialized on each reference.

Deferred query execution provides an opportunity for changing the values of parameters between query invocations. Consider defining a variable locationOfInterest and a query expression filmsAtLocation that returns the films filmed at the locationOfInterest:

```
var locationOfInterest = "Phoenix";
var filmsAtLocation =
    from      f in filmProjects
    where     f.Location == locationOfInterest
    select    f;
```

The first time that filmsAtLocation is referenced it returns the films filmed in "Phoenix". If the value of the variable locationOfInterest is changed to "San Diego", then a subsequent reference to filmsAtLocation returns San Diego films.

Note that there are some query operators that force the immediate execution of a query, such as the operators that return a scalar value (e.g., Average, Count, Max, Min, Sum) or a single element of a collection (e.g., First, Last, Single). The query developer can also force immediate execution of any query by materializing the query using a conversion operator, such as ToArray or ToList, to cache the results in the designated data structure. These materialized results can then be reused for subsequent query references provided that the underlying data on which the materialized query depends has not changed. Otherwise, the materialized results would be out of date.

2.5.1.7 Checkpoint: LINQ

LINQ provides a declarative object-based query language within the .NET Framework. This section illustrated how to use LINQ to query collections of objects. LINQ can also be used to query collections of relational tuples or collections of XML elements. The syntax is essentially the same. For relational databases, once the connection to the database is established, the attributes are accessed using familiar dot notation. For XML, after loading the XML document, the methods Descendants and Elements return a collection of elements for querying. LINQ also provides a programmer with a declarative language for programming in C#.

LINQ uses a combination of the more familiar from-where-select query comprehension syntax in combination with query operators. Table 2.2 provides a summary of the common query operators discussed in this section.

Table 2.2: Summary of LINQ Query Operators.	
Purpose	**Query Operators**
Set Membership and Quantification	All, Any, Contains
Accessing Elements	First, Last, Single, Take
Sets	Distinct, Except, Intersect, Union
Aggregation	Average, Count, Max, Min, Sum

2.5.2   DB4O

The db4o open-source OODB is a simple yet powerful system that is typically used as an embeddable standalone database, although it also supports a client/server mode. db4o is cross-platform and works with both the C# and Java OOPLs. It supports the ACID transaction properties as well as replication and synchronization of objects. db4o is typically used in application areas that have data consisting of complex object structures where data typically belongs to the application.

The db4o database takes a simpler approach for persistence than the approach represented by the ODMG standard and other OODB products that use an ODL-like schema specification compiled into language-specific bindings for a particular OOPL. db4o does not have a separate schema specification. Any class defined in the OOPL can be stored in the database explicitly using the db4o API.

The use of db4o requires either adding a reference to the dynamic link library (dll) for C# or adding the Java archive (jar file) to the classpath for Java. In addition, the Db4objects.Db4o namespace (package) must also be used (imported). This case study will continue to use the C# language for examples and to use the method names as documented in the 7.12 version of db4o for the .NET Framework 3.5, which supports LINQ. Typically, the only difference between the db4o API method names is the case of the initial letter, as C# uses *PascalCase* with an initial uppercase letter and Java uses *camelCase* with an initial lowercase letter.

To create a db4o database, first open a database file using the Db4oFactory class as shown:

IObjectContainer db = Db4oFactory.OpenFile("Hollywood.yap");

An IObjectContainer represents the db4o database, and the variable db provides a reference to the database. Each IObjectContainer manages object identity and has its own transaction. The opening of the database represents the start of a transaction. When the database is closed using db.Close(), the transaction is committed. To define a transaction scope with a finer granularity than that provided by the opening and closing of the database, try-catch blocks can be used to commit a completed transaction or to rollback the transaction when an exception occurs using the Commit() and Rollback() methods of the IObjectContainer.

```
try
{
            database operations here
}
catch (Exception e)
{
            db.Rollback();
}
finally
{
            db.Commit();
}
```

Storing objects in the database uses the Store method of the db4o API, which was known as the Set() method in earlier versions of db4o. Once an object is constructed in main memory, it can be explicitly stored in the database. For example, assuming that the variable model111 references a non-null Model object in main memory, then db.Store(model111) stores the object model111 and any objects that it references in the database, if the referenced object is not already stored in the db4o database.

The db4o system provides several ways to retrieve objects from the database, which requires the use of the Db4objects.Db4o.Query namespace (package). One method uses a *Query By Example* (QBE) mechanism to retrieve objects based on a template object. For example, to find a film project located in "Phoenix", a template object is created with a location of "Phoenix" with default values for the remaining properties (null for objects and 0 for numeric fields):

```
FilmProject phxFilmTemplate =
            new FilmProject {
                    Location = "Phoenix",
                    ProjectId = null,
                    Cost = 0,
                    Title = null,
                    Type = null };
    IObjectSet result = db.QueryByExample(phxFilmTemplate);
```

This example shows the object initialization feature of the .NET Framework allowing for initializing an object's properties by name rather than by position. The QueryByExample method, Get() in earlier versions, returns a set of objects that match the template object. The programming language can then be used to iterate through the result set.

Another method to retrieve objects in db4o is to use *native* queries, which are queries expressed in the programming language. Since LINQ is seamlessly integrated into the C# language, LINQ can be used to declaratively query a db4o database natively. Using LINQ with db4o requires adding a reference to the Db4objects.Db4o.Linq.dll to the project and the following using statements to the program:

```
using System.Linq;
using Db4objects.Db4o.Linq;
```

Therefore, this exposition will assume the use of LINQ for querying a db4o database rather than detailing the API of the native query interface.

Earlier in this case study, the capabilities of LINQ were explored in the context of the HOL-LYWOOD ENTERPRISE. Assuming that the classes have been implemented according to the UML class diagram specified in Figure 2.4 and that there is an extent defined for each class, all of the queries in Section 2.5.1 can be used with db4o. The Query method from the native query API can be used to define extent names for use with the LINQ queries. For example, db.Query<Model>() retrieves all Model objects in the database. Therefore, a named extent for models can be defined using the following LINQ query:

```
var models = from m in db.Query<Model>() select m;
```

Updating objects in the database requires first retrieving the object to be updated, updating the fields, and then storing the object back in the database. The following code snippet illustrates how to update the phone number of a model whose PId value is "444444444".

```
var modelOfInterest =
        (from m in models where m.PId == "444444444" select m).Single();
modelOfInterest.Phone = "123-456-7890";
db.Store(modelOfInterest);
```

The retrieval of the object binds the variable to the appropriate object reference so that the subsequent storage updates the object in the database. Without first establishing the reference, db4o cannot distinguish between storing a new object versus updating an existing object.

Deleting objects in db4o follows a similar pattern, in that, the object to be deleted must first be retrieved from the database to establish the object reference. Then a call to the Delete method deletes the object from the database. Using the call db.Delete(modelOfInterest), instead of Store in the preceding update example, would result in deleting the model from the database.

This quick overview illustrates how to get started using the db4o OODB. However, the population, update, and delete of an object database with complex objects and associations is not trivial. The initial population as well as subsequent modifications to the database must validate the associations between objects as part of the behavior of the object. For example, the binary association representing movie stars appearing in film projects must be consistent, ensuring that an actor in the film's Actors property has the film in the ActsIn property of the movie star.

2.6   CHECKPOINT

Object-oriented databases are an alternative data model to that provided by the traditional relational data model. An object-oriented data model more closely represents the enterprises expressed in an object-oriented conceptual data model, such as an EER or UML diagram. The ODMG standard provides a data definition language and declarative query language that forms a foundation for the discussion and portability of object-oriented databases. The case study illustrated the features of LINQ and how LINQ can be used as a declarative query language within an OODB implementation using the db4o open-source database, which provides an embeddable, standalone system supporting object persistence with transactions.

2.7   BIBLIOGRAPHIC REFERENCES

The Object Data Standard [Cattell et al., 2000] was developed to provide a common ground to describe an object model, the specification of a schema over the object model, and a query language. There are also several books available that are a collection of papers describing the use of object-oriented databases in practice [Loomis and Chaudhri, 1997] and [Chaudhri and Zicari, 2000]. The ODBMS.ORG portal [ODBMS.ORG, 2010] provides free resources for object databases. There are multiple resources available on the LINQ language, from articles for database educators [Dietrich and Chaudhari, 2009] to books for putting LINQ into practice [Calvert and Kulkarni, 2009, Marguerie et al., 2008]. There is a lightweight interactive development available for LINQ, known as LINQPad [Albahari, 2010], which provides a straightforward environment for using LINQ. The open-source db4o database is available on the Web [Versant, 2010], and there are other sources that document its use and applicability in applications [Edlich et al., 2006].

CHAPTER 3

Object-Relational Databases

Since the introduction of the first commercial relational database products in the early 1980's, relational database technology has become a multi-billion dollar business. During this growth period, the practical use of relational technology for more complex, non-business-oriented applications was challenged in the wake of the object-oriented database movement. Users began to experiment with the use of relational databases in applications that required data types above and beyond the simple built-in data types provided by most commercial systems. These non-traditional applications typically involved large amounts of data, such as video, audio, and spatial data, and/or complex, hierarchically structured data, such as designs of engineering artifacts. Researchers subsequently began to investigate ways to incorporate object-oriented concepts, such as those covered in Chapter 1, into relational database systems, creating object-relational database technology. Whereas, object-oriented database technology provides a *revolutionary* approach that requires the construction of new object storage and server facilities, object-relational database technology provides an *evolutionary* approach to the use of objects in databases by building on established relational database research results. Today, the SQL standard captures many of these original concepts as object extensions to the relational standard, with companies such as Oracle, IBM, Informix, and Sybase providing object-relational products, also known as *universal servers*.

This chapter presents the object features of the SQL standard and the manner in which such features have been incorporated into the Oracle commercial database product. A fundamental concept supporting object extensions to the relational model is that of *extensibility* through the use of *user-defined data types (UDTs)*. UDTs allow application developers to go beyond the built-in data types of the relational model, defining more complex, structured data types that are appropriate to the application at hand. UDTs in the SQL standard fully support the object-oriented concept of encapsulation, where users can define methods for manipulating the instances of a UDT. UDTs can also be formed into inheritance hierarchies, supporting inheritance of attributes and methods as well as the object-oriented concepts of polymorphism and overriding of method implementations. A UDT can then be used in the same way as any other built-in data type: for defining the types of columns in tables, for defining parameters, or for defining variables in SQL routines.

Although UDTs can be used strictly as a means for creating more complex column, variable, or parameter *values*, UDTs also provide the basis for the creation of *objects*. UDTs can be used together with a new form of table known as a *typed table*. When a typed table is formed based on a UDT, the rows of the typed table become objects, with object identifiers that are referred to as *references*. References can then be used to create object-based associations between typed tables in the same way that object relationships are formed between classes in an object-oriented database. Coupling the use of object references with the array data type of the SQL standard also supports the creation of multivalued object associations, providing an intuitive way to model 1:N and M:N associations between objects. Typed tables can also be formed into an inheritance hierarchy that corresponds to the hierarchy of the UDTs on which they are based, thus supporting object inheritance.

This chapter begins with a discussion of the SQL built-in *constructed types*, such as row types and arrays, for the construction of more complex values. Although the built-in constructed types are not part of the object features of the standard, they are useful in support of mapping object-oriented conceptual models to object-relational representations. The chapter then addresses constructed types in the form of UDTs, illustrating how UDTs and typed tables can be used to take an object-oriented approach to the design of relational databases. Techniques for mapping EER and UML models to the object-relational features of the SQL standard are then addressed, followed by a case study of the object-relational features of Oracle 11g.

3.1   BUILT-IN CONSTRUCTED TYPES

In addition to atomic types, such as character, integer, real, and Boolean, the SQL standard supports a category of data type known as *constructed types*, consisting of *user-defined types (UDTs)*, a *reference type*, a *row type*, and a *collection type*. Constructed types are data types that are capable of holding more than one value. Row types and collection types are built-in data types, while UDTs and reference types provide a user-defined approach to extending the built-in types that are available in relational database systems.

This section provides an overview of the built-in row and collection types. Row types and collection types will be used later in this chapter to support the mapping of object-oriented conceptual models to object-relational implementations. Since UDTs and reference types are the main topic of this chapter, each of these constructed types are covered in more detail in separate sections.

Examples are presented using the School Database Enterprise in Figure 3.1. As shown in Figure 3.1, each instance of Person has a pId, dob, firstName, and lastName, where pId is the primary key. Because of the total and disjoint specialization relationship between Person, Student, and Faculty, a Person *must* be either a Student or a Faculty member, but not both. Each Student has a status (freshman, sophomore, junior, senior), and each Faculty has a rank (assistant professor, associate professor, professor).

A Department has two attributes: a code and a name, with code being the primary key. Each Student and Faculty instance must be associated with a Department through the majorsIn or worksIn relationship, respectively. A Department can have a Faculty instance as the department chair through the chair relationship. Each Faculty member can serve as the chair of at most one Department. A Faculty instance can only be the chair of the Department in which he/she works.

Each CampusClub has a cId, a name, a location, and a phoneNumber, where cId is the primary key. A Student can optionally be a member of many CampusClub organizations. Likewise, a CampusClub can have many Student members. A CampusClub can have a Faculty member as an advisor. Each Faculty member can advise many CampusClub organizations.

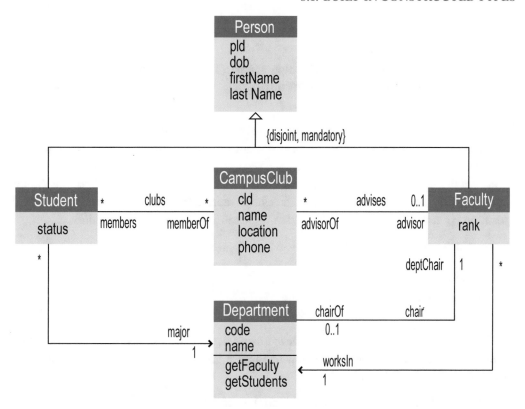

Figure 3.1: UML Diagram of the SCHOOL DATABASE. From *Succeeding with Object Databases* by Akmal B. Chaudri and Roberto Zicari. Copyright ©2000 by Akmal B. Chaudri and Roberto Zicari. All rights reserved. Reproduced here by permission of Wiley Publishing, Inc.

3.1.1   ROW TYPES

A traditional relational table is composed of rows with the distinguishing characteristic that each column value in each row must be atomic, which is the basic definition of first normal form (1NF). The SQL standard relaxes the 1NF requirement with the introduction of the row type. The row type allows a row to be stored as a column value inside of another row.

Using the SCHOOL DATABASE ENTERPRISE in Figure 3.1, suppose the location of a campus club consists of a street name, building name, and room number. These three values could be represented as three separate columns in a table. Using a row type, however, the location of a club can be conceptually viewed as one column with a non-atomic value. Each element of the column is referred to as a *field*. In the example below, location is identified as a row type with the keyword row, followed by field name and type pairs enclosed in parentheses and separated by commas.

```
create table campusClub
(  cId       varchar(10),
   name      varchar(50) not null,
   location  row (street varchar(30), bldg varchar(5), room varchar(5)),
   advisor   varchar(11) references faculty(pId),
   primary key (cId));
```

The row constructor is used to assign values to the fields of a row. The values in the row constructor can either be a list of values or the result of a query. In either case, the types of the values must conform to the field types in the row type definition. The following example illustrates inserting a club into the campusClub table, where the club is located in Room 222 of the Brickyard Building on Mill Avenue. The location of the club is represented as one column in the table, but the location is a non-atomic value composed of three separate character string values.

```
insert into campusClub values
(  'CC123',
   'Campus Computer Club',
   row('Mill Avenue', 'Brickyard Building', 'Rm 222'),
   'FA123');
```

The values of a row type can be retrieved using dot notation to access the individual fields that are part of the column. The query below will return the street, building, and room number for the location of the specified club.

```
select    c.location.street, c.location.bldg, c.location.room
from      campusClub c
where     c.name = 'Campus Computer Club';
```

3.1.2   ARRAYS AS COLLECTIONS

The collection type provides an additional way to represent non-atomic values in a relational schema. Theoretically, a collection can be a structure such as an array, a set, a list, or a bag, but the current version of the SQL standard only supports the array type.

A column in a table can be specified as an array by following the column type with the array keyword. The maximum number of elements in an array is enclosed in square brackets. The first position in an array is accessed with an index value of one.

Again using the campusClub table as an example, a members array can be used to directly store the identifiers of the club members inside of each row of the campusClub table.

```
create table campusClub
(  cId       varchar(10),
   name      varchar(50) not null,
   location  row (street varchar(30), bldg varchar(5), room varchar(5)),
   advisor   varchar(9) references faculty(pId),
```

```
members varchar(11) array[50] references student(pId),
primary key (cId));
```

The array constructor is used to reserve space for an array and can also be used to assign values to the array elements. The following insert statement illustrates how to initialize the members array to an empty value using the array constructor with no elements.

```
insert into campusClub values
(  'CC123',
   'Campus Computer Club',
   row('Mill Avenue', 'Brickyard Building', 'Rm 222'),
   'FA123',
   array[ ]);
```

The specific identifiers of club members can then be added to the array by using the array constructor in an update statement. The following statement assigns values to the first three positions in the members array.

```
update    campusClub
set       members = array['ST111', 'ST222', 'ST333']
where     name = 'Campus Computer Club';
```

Assignments can also be made to individual positions in an array by using a specific index value.

```
update    campusClub
set       members[4] = 'ST444'
where     name = 'Campus Computer Club';
```

An index is used to access a specific position of an array. The following query returns the identifier of the second element of the members array for the specified club.

```
select    members[2]
from      campusClub
where     name = 'Campus Computer Club';
```

The cardinality function can be used to get the size of an array. For example, cardinality(c.members) returns the current size of the members array (assuming c is a cursor to a row in the campusClub table.). The cardinality function can be used to support iteration through array contents within SQL routines.

The cardinality of an array is adjustable, ranging from an empty array to the maximum size specified in the array definition. Given the four values that were assigned to the array in the previous examples, the current cardinality of the array is four. Suppose an additional update statement sets position six to the value 'ST666'. Then the cardinality of the array becomes six, with position five set to null.

In general, arrays are useful for representing multivalued attributes. Arrays can also be used to directly model the many side of a 1:N or M:N association as in the use of relationships in ODL. In the remainder of this chapter, arrays will be used to illustrate a more object-oriented approach to the representation of multivalued relationships in an object-relational schema.

3.1.3   CHECKPOINT: BUILT-IN CONSTRUCTED TYPES

Row types and arrays extend the pure relational model with capabilities for representing non-atomic values in table columns. Row types are useful for representing composite values, where each component of the row type is of a possibly different data type. Arrays can be used to represent an indexed collection of values with a homogeneous data type.

3.2   USER-DEFINED TYPES

The term *user-defined type (UDT)* is the SQL standard terminology for *abstract data type*. Most readers should already be familiar with the concept of abstract data types, where users define new types having some form of internal structure together with methods that represent the behavior of the type. The internal representation of the type is *encapsulated* by the behavior of the type, meaning that the internal implementation of the type is hidden from the outside world and can even change without affecting the manner in which a user interfaces with the type. UDTs in the SQL standard are somewhat different from the strict definition of an abstract data type since all internal attributes of a UDT and their associated methods are public and cannot be marked as protected or private as in languages such as Java or C++. The primary advantage of a UDT is that it allows database developers to define new application-oriented types, above and beyond built-in atomic and constructed types, that can be used in the definition of relational tables. UDTs also provide the basis for the creation of objects in the relational world.

This section describes the two basic types of UDT in the SQL standard: the *distinct type* and the *structured type*. The syntax for defining a UDT using the **create type** statement is presented in Figure 3.2. The details of the syntax will be addressed in the subsections that follow.

3.2.1   DISTINCT TYPES

A distinct type provides a way of attaching special meaning to an existing atomic type. Once a distinct type is defined, use of the type cannot be freely mixed with the atomic type on which it is based. The distinct type essentially defines a new form of the atomic type.

As an example, suppose you need a table that maintains the age and weight of each person in a database. You could always define columns for `personAge` and `personWeight` that are of type `integer`. You could then add the age and weight of the person, since both values are of the same type, even though the addition of the two values is meaningless.

```
create type <user_defined_type_body>

<user_defined_type_body> ::= <user_defined_type_name>
    [under <user_defined_type_name>]
    [as <representation>]
    [ [not] instantiable]
    [not] final
    [ref is system generated | ref using <predefined type> | ref from <attribute_name> [{,attribute_name}...]]
    [<method_specification_list>]

<representation> ::= <predefined_type> | <member_list>

<member_list> ::= (<attribute_definition> [{, <attribute_definition>} ...])

<attribute_definition> ::= <attribute_name> {<data_type> | <collection_type>}
    [<reference_scope_check>] [default <default_value>]

<data_type> ::= <predefined_type> | <reference_type>

<collection_type> ::= <data_type> array [unsigned_integer]      /* [ ] part of syntax*/

<method_specification_list> ::= <method_specification> [{ ,<method_specification>}...]

<method_specification> ::= <partial_method_specification> | <overriding_method_specification>

<overriding_method_specification> ::= overriding <partial_method_specification>

<partial_method_specification> ::= [constructor] method <method_name>
    <SQL_parameter_declarations>
    returns <data_type>
```

Figure 3.2: SQL Syntax for Creating User-Defined Types

To prevent meaningless calculations with values that are of the same type but conceptually have different semantics, distinct types can be defined using the create type statement in Figure 3.2. In the example below, age and weight are defined as two different distinct types, both based on the integer atomic type using the as clause of the create type statement.

```
create type age as integer final;
create type weight as integer final;
```

```
create table person
(  personId        varchar(3),
   personAge       age,
   personWeight    weight,
   primary key (personId));
```

The keyword final is required syntax for distinct types in the current version of the SQL standard and simply means that a subtype of the distinct type cannot be defined. The distinct types in the example are then used to define the personAge and personWeight columns, respectively.

Once defined, age and weight values cannot be compared. In fact, age and weight values cannot be mixed with the regular integer type since age, weight, and integer are conceptually different types.

As an example of using distinct types, the following query retrieves the personId values of each person having an age less than the age of the person with a personId of '123'.

```
select     p1.personId
from       person p1, person p2
where      p2.personId = '123' and p1.personAge < p2.personAge;
```

The following query is invalid since it mixes the use of age, weight, and integer values.

```
select     personId
from       person
where      (personAge * 2) < personWeight;
```

Mixing the use of distinct types with the atomic types on which they are based is allowed, but it requires the deliberate use of the cast function. The invalid query above can be revised as shown below to cast all values to the integer type, thus transforming the condition in the where clause into a valid condition.

```
select     personId
from       person
where      cast (personAge as integer) * 2 < cast (personWeight as integer);
```

Methods can also be defined on distinct types to create specialized operations for manipulating and comparing distinct types. Rather than elaborate on the use of methods with distinct types, the next section discusses the use of methods in the context of structured types.

3.2.2   STRUCTURED TYPES

Whereas a distinct type creates a new type from one specific atomic type, a structured type is a UDT that is composed of several internal components. Each internal component can be of a different type. An instance of a structured type is a value, but since a structured type can contain several components, the value is a composite value.

As a simple example of a structured type definition, recall the previous example of defining a campus club location as a row type. Instead of using a row type, a structured type can be used. In the example below, locationUdt is defined as a structured type.

```
create type locationUdt as
(   street    varchar(30),
    bldg      varchar(5),
    room      varchar(5))
    not final;
```

The representation of the type in the as clause defines the type to contain the street, bldg, and room components. These components are the *attributes* of the structured type, where the type of each attribute can be a built-in atomic or a constructed type as well as any user-defined type. The keywords not final are referred to as the *finality* clause of the type definition. In a structured type definition, the finality clause must always be not final (a current restriction of the SQL standard), indicating that it is possible to define subtypes of the type. Type hierarchies will be discussed in more detail later in this chapter.

The example below uses locationUdt to define the type of the location column in the campusClub table.

```
create table campusClub
(   cld           varchar(10),
    name          varchar(50) not null,
    location      locationUdt,
    advisor       varchar(11) references faculty(pld),
    members       varchar(11) array[50] references student(pld),
    primary key (cld));
```

3.2.2.1 Built-In Methods

In the SQL standard, there are three types of stored procedures: functions, procedures, and methods. Methods are specifically associated with structured types. In particular, methods are functions that are tightly bound to the definition of the structured type. Structured types therefore support encapsulation, where the type is manipulated only through the methods that are defined on the type. In the SQL standard, methods cannot be defined as procedures. Specific implementations of structured types, however, such as that found in Oracle, allow methods to be defined as functions or procedures (see the Oracle object-relational case study within this chapter).

There are three types of built-in methods for structured types: a *constructor function*, *observer functions*, and *mutator functions*. These methods are automatically provided as part of the type definition. The constructor function has the same name as the type and is used for creating instances of the type. The constructor function must always be invoked using the new expression. Observer functions are used for retrieving the attribute values of a structured type. There is an observer function for every attribute of the type, where the function has the same name as the attribute. In a similar manner, mutator functions are used to modify the attribute values of a structured type. There is a mutator function for every attribute of the type having the same name as the attribute. Observer functions and mutator functions are always invoked using dot notation (variable.functionName) instead of using traditional functional notation (functionName(parameters)). Traditional functional notation is only used for functions that are not methods.

The next example illustrates a sequence of code from an SQL routine that uses the constructor function and mutator functions to create an instance of locationUdt.

```
begin
      declare loc locationUdt;
      set loc = new locationUdt();        /* invoking the constructor function */
      set loc.street = 'Mill Avenue';     /* invoking the mutator functions */
      set loc.bldg = 'Brickyard Building';
      set loc.room = 'RM 222';
      insert into campusClub values
               (  'CC123',
                  'Campus Computer Club',
                  loc, /* initializing location */
                  'FA123',
                  array[]);
end;
```

The code defines the variable loc to be of type locationUdt. The variable is then initialized with a new instance by using new locationUdt() to invoke the constructor function. This system-defined constructor function has no parameters. The new instance of the type has all of its attribute values set to either null or to a default value that can be specified in the type definition. In our current use of structured types, it is important to understand that the new instance is a *value* and not an *object*. Using structured types together with typed tables to create objects will be addressed in more detail later in this chapter.

Mutator functions are invoked for each attribute of the instance to assign values to each attribute. For example, loc.street invokes the mutator function for street to assign the value 'Mill Avenue' to the attribute. There are actually two parameters to any mutator function. The first parameter is implicit and is the instance of the type. In this example, the implicit parameter is the instance stored in the loc variable. The second parameter is explicit and is the value assigned to the attribute ('Mill Avenue' for the street mutator function). The value returned by a mutator function is a new instance of the type with the modified attribute value. The loc variable is then used in the insert statement to assign the location value to the location column of a row in the campusClub table.

The query below illustrates the use of observer functions to retrieve the attribute values of the structured type. For example, c.location.street invokes the street observer function to access the value of the street attribute. Similar to mutator functions, the instance of the type is an implicit parameter of the function. Mutator functions, however, have no explicit parameters. The value returned by the mutator function is the value of the attribute that it accesses.

```
select    name, c.location.street, c.location.bldg, c.location.room
from      campusClub c
where     name = 'Campus Computer Club';
```

Because of potential naming ambiguities in SQL, structured types and observer functions can only be accessed through the use of alias names in queries (i.e., c in the previous query). As a result, a reference such as location.street or campusClub.location.street is not allowed.

3.2.2.2   User-Defined Methods

In addition to built-in methods, users can define their own methods on structured types, which is one of the main advantages of UDTs. The syntax for the create type statement in Figure 3.2 indicates an option for a method specification list. The method specification list is where the user defines the *signature* of each method, indicating the name of each method together with the names and types of its parameters. The implementation of the method is defined separately from the type specification using the create method statement.

The example below illustrates the definition of the sum method on the threeNumbers structured type. The signature indicates that this particular method has no explicit parameters defined. The method also returns a value of type integer. Every method, however, has one implicit parameter, which is the instance of the type on which the method is defined. The value of the implicit parameter is accessed in the method implementation using the self keyword.

```
create type threeNumbers as
(  one        integer,
   two        integer,
   three      integer)
   not final
   method sum() returns integer;
create method sum() returns integer for threeNumbers
begin
   return self.one + self.two + self.three;
end
```

Users can override the constructor function of a structured type. Since the system-defined constructor function does not allow parameters, overriding the constructor function creates a different version of the constructor function that can be used to set the values of specific attributes at the time an instance of the type is created.

The example below illustrates overriding the constructor function of the locationUdt type. As indicated in the syntax of Figure 3.2, the keyword overriding must be specified to indicate that the method is overriding an existing function.

```
create type locationUdt as
( street      varchar(30),
  bldg        varchar(5),
  room        varchar(5))
  not final
  overriding constructor method locationUdt /* new constructor with parameters */
              (street varchar(30), bldg varchar(5), room varchar(5)) returns locationUdt;
create method locationUdt(st varchar(30), bl varchar(5), rm varchar(5))
  returns locationUdt for locationUdt
begin
  set self.street = st;
  set self.bldg = bl;
  set self.room = rm;
  return self;
end;
```

Since the method to be overridden is also a constructor function, the **constructor** keyword must be specified. The name of the method must be the same as the name of the system-defined constructor function (i.e., locationUdt)). The method specification includes the definition of parameters and their types. The method implementation demonstrates the manner in which the parameters are used to assign values to an instance of the type using the mutator functions. Notice that the method returns self as a value, which is the modified instance of locationUdt.

The user-defined constructor function can then be used to construct a new instance of locationUdt and to set the values of its attributes at the same time.

```
declare loc locationUdt;
set loc = new locationUdt('Mill Avenue', 'Brickyard Building', 'Rm 222');
```

3.2.3   CHECKPOINT: USER-DEFINED TYPES

User-defined types allow database programmers to extend the built-in SQL data types to define new types that are appropriate for a specific application. Distinct types provide a way to rename a built-in type for the purpose of attaching special meaning to the type. Structured types allow the definition of a composite type, supporting the specification of methods that are tightly bound to the type for manipulation and access purposes. Structured types automatically provide a constructor method as well as accessor and mutator methods for each component of the structured type.

3.3   TYPED TABLES

As described in the previous section, an instance of a UDT in the SQL standard is a value. To create the notion of an object as in object-oriented database technology, a UDT must be used together with a *typed table*. A typed table is a new form of table in the SQL standard that is always associated with a specific structured type. A typed table has a column for every attribute of the structured type on which it is based. In addition, a typed table has a *self-referencing column* that contains a unique object identifier, known as a *reference*, for each row in the table. Other than the self-referencing column and the attributes of the structured type, additional columns cannot be added to the table definition.

When a structured type is used to define a typed table, an instance of the type is viewed as an object, with the self-referencing column providing the object identifier. Unlike object identifiers in object-oriented database technology, an object identifier is only unique within a specific typed table. As a result, it is possible to have two typed tables with rows that have identical self-referencing values.

As an example of using typed tables, suppose you would like to implement the Department class of the School Database Enterprise in Figure 3.1 as a typed table. It is first necessary to define a departmentUdt structured type.

```
create type departmentUdt as
(   code          varchar(3),
    name          varchar(40))
    instantiable not final ref is system generated;
```

The departmentUdt type defines the code and name attributes. A new syntactic feature from Figure 3.2 introduced in the type definition is the instantiable clause. The instantiable clause indicates that a constructor function exists for the type and that it is possible for the user to directly create instances of the type. If a type is specified as not instantiable, then there is no constructor function for the type. The use of not instantiable only makes sense in the context of a type that has a subtype, where instances of the type are created at the subtype level only. Type hierarchies are addressed in more detail in the next section. A structured type that is used together with a typed table as in the example of this section must always be specified as instantiable.

Another new feature introduced in the type definition is the ref is system generated clause. This clause allows the user to specify the means for generating the value for the object reference. As indicated in Figure 3.2, the object reference can either be *system generated*, *user defined*, or *derived*. If the reference is system generated, then the database system is responsible for generating a unique object reference for instances of the type. If the reference is user defined, then the user must provide a unique reference for each instance of the type, where the value of the reference is the type indicated in the ref using clause. If the reference is derived, then the user must specify the list of attributes from the structured type that will be used to provide a unique object reference. For user defined and derived references, it is the user's responsibility to ensure the uniqueness of the reference. The examples in this chapter use system generated references since this is the most natural approach to take for the use of objects.

Once the departmentUdt is defined, a typed table that corresponds to the structured type is defined.

```
create table department of departmentUdt
(   primary key (code),
    ref is departmentID system generated);
```

The syntax for creating typed tables is shown in Figure 3.3. The of clause indicates the structured type on which the typed table is based. As a result, the table automatically acquires columns that correspond to the attributes of the structured type. The typed table definition supports the same table and column constraints that are associated with regular table definitions. For example, in the department table definition, the code attribute of departmentUdt is defined as a primary key. Other constraints such as unique or not null can also be specified using either the column or table constraint format. Only the attributes with constraints are listed in the typed table definition.

According to the syntax in Figure 3.3, a typed table definition must also repeat a reference generation specification that is consistent with the reference generation specification of the structured type. In addition, the ref is specification must assign a name to the self referencing column. This name (departmentID) can be used to manipulate the self-referencing column in the case of user-defined references. The self-referencing column is also used to access the self-referencing value. Accessing the self-referencing column will be described in a following section on the use of reference types for establishing object-to-object relationships.

create table <table name> of <user_defined_type_name> [under <supertable_name> [<table_element_list>]]

<table_element_list> ::= (<table_element> [{ ,<table_element>}...])

<table_element> ::= <table_constraint> | <self_referencing_column_specification> | <column_options>

<self_referencing_column_specification> ::= ref is <self_referencing_column_name> <reference_generation>

<reference_generation> ::= system generated | user generated | derived

<column_options> ::= <column_name> with options <column_option_list>

<column_option_list> ::= [scope <table_name> [<reference_scope_check>]] [default <default_value>]
    [<column_constraint>...]

Figure 3.3: SQL Syntax for Creating Typed Tables

Rows are inserted into a typed table using an insert statement in the same manner as for any relational table. Consider the following insert statements for department.

insert into department values ('cse', 'Computer Science and Engineering');
insert into department values ('ece', 'Electrical and Computer Engineering');
insert into department values ('mae', 'Mechanical and Aerospace Engineering');

The resulting rows of the table are as shown in Table 3.1, where the values for the self-referencing column are system generated. If the reference is user-defined, the insert statement must include the value for the self-referencing column. If the reference is derived from attributes of the type, the primary key constraint or the unique and not null constraints can be used in the table definition to ensure a unique reference value for the appropriate attributes.

Table 3.1: Rows in the department Typed Table.		
(self-referencing column) **departmentID**	**code**	**name**
10287534556	cse	Computer Science and Engineering
27259489035	ece	Electrical and Computer Engineering
90324854948	mae	Mechanical and Aerospace Engineering

3.4   TYPE AND TABLE HIERARCHIES

Structured types and typed tables can be formed into hierarchies to directly represent the super-class/subclass hierarchies of conceptual models such as the EER model and UML class diagrams. Structured types are first formed into a hierarchy using the under clause as specified in the syntax for the create type statement in Figure 3.2. The under clause allows the specification of the supertype of the type being defined. Creating a supertype/subtype relationship between structured types fully supports the inheritance of attributes and methods of the supertype at the subtype level. Typed tables are then created to correspond to the type hierarchy, also using an under clause as specified in Figure 3.3 for the syntax of typed table specifications. Inheritance is also supported among the object instances of typed tables.

As an example of creating type and table hierarchies, the SCHOOL DATABASE ENTERPRISE in Figure 3.1 provides a Person superclass with the Student and Faculty subclasses. Appendix A illustrates several techniques for mapping such a hierarchy to traditional relational tables. Typed tables, however, can be used in object-relational technology to directly represent the hierarchy, to provide object identifiers for the data associated with the hierarchy, and to directly support inheritance of attributes and methods. Structured type definitions are first created for the Person, Student, and Faculty classes from Figure 3.1.

```
create type personUdt as
( pId            varchar(11),
  firstName      varchar(20),
  lastName       varchar(20),
  dob            date)
  instantiable not final ref is system generated;
create type facultyUdt under personUdt as
( rank           varchar(10))
  instantiable
  not final;
```

```
create type studentUdt under personUdt as
(  status          varchar(10))
   instantiable
   not final;
```

To form the hierarchy, facultyUdt is defined as a subtype of personUdt with the under personUdt clause. In a similar manner, studentUdt is defined as under personUdt, indicating that studentUdt is a subtype of personUdt. Recall that structured types must always be defined as not final. Furthermore, since these types are intended to be used with typed tables, the instantiable clause is required.

As a result of the supertype/subtype relationship between personUdt and facultyUdt, an instance of facultyUdt will inherit the pId, firstName, lastName, and dob attributes as well as the mutator and accessor functions associated with each attribute. An instance of facultyUdt will therefore have five attributes: the four inherited attributes as well as the rank attribute that is directly defined at the facultyUdt level. If the personUdt type had any additional user-defined methods, these methods would also be inherited by facultyUdt. The same inheritance situation exists for the supertype/subtype relationship that exists between personUdt and studentUdt.

With the person type hierarchy defined, typed tables can be created that directly correspond to the type hierarchy. The example that follows illustrates the manner in which the person, faculty, and student typed tables are defined. The under specification of the subtables must be consistent with the under specification of the corresponding types. For example, facultyUdt was defined to be under personUdt. Since the person table is associated with the personUdt type and the faculty table is associated with the facultyUdt type, then faculty must be defined to be under person. The same constraints hold for the definition of the student table.

```
create table person of personUdt
(  primary key (pId),
   ref is personID system generated);
create table faculty of facultyUdt under person;
create table student of studentUdt under person;
```

There are several rules associated with the definition of type and table hierarchies. In each case, only single inheritance is supported. As a result, every subtype/subtable must have only one maximal supertype/supertable. A primary key can only be defined for a maximal supertable. In the person table hierarchy, pId is identified as a primary key only within the person table. The primary key is inherited by all of the subtables. Subtables can indirectly define keys through the use of the not null and unique constraints.

A self-referencing column can only be defined at the supertype/supertable level. Referring again to the personUdt type hierarchy and the person table hierarchy, the ref is clause is only used in the personUdt type definition and the person table definition. The self-referencing column is inherited by all subtables of person.

An additional rule is associated with the definition of constraints in typed tables. Column and table constraints can only be defined on *originally-defined attributes* and not on inherited attributes.

Originally-defined attributes are the attributes introduced in the structured type on which the table is based. For example, rank is an originally-defined attribute of the faculty table. As a result, the table definition could be modified to place a not null constraint on rank, but not on an inherited attribute such as lastName.

Although this section has introduced type hierarchies in parallel with the use of table hierarchies, it is important to understand that type hierarchies can be used independently of table hierarchies. In this case, use of the type hierarchy supports valued-based inheritance rather than object-based inheritance. Furthermore, the use of the not instantiable clause can only be used in type hierarchies that are not associated with typed tables. For example, a user can define a supertype A as not instantiable and then define B and C as instantiable subtypes of A. Since A is not instantiable, users cannot directly create instances of A but can directly create instances of B and C that inherit the attributes and methods of A.

All types associated with a typed table hierarchy *must* be defined as instantiable. As a result, abstract supertables and the total specialization constraint cannot be inherently enforced.

3.5 A CLOSER LOOK AT TABLE HIERARCHIES

The advantage of table hierarchies is that they support the same form of object-based inheritance as found in class hierarchies in object-oriented database systems. As a result, object-relational applications can directly model superclass/subclass hierarchies from conceptual models, where the rows of typed tables are actual objects with object identifiers. This section demonstrates the insertion of rows in a table hierarchy, the inheritance behavior of rows in a table hierarchy, and the manner in which such rows are queried and manipulated in SQL.

3.5.1 INSERTING ROWS IN A TABLE HIERARCHY

Inserting a row in a table hierarchy is similar to the creation of objects in a class hierarchy of an object-oriented database. Each row has a most specific table that defines the type of the row. This type corresponds to the type of the table in which the row is directly inserted. Inserting a row in a table makes the row visible in all supertables of the table. The row is not visible, however, in any of the subtables of the table. Once inserted, a row cannot migrate to other tables in the hierarchy. The most specific type/table of a row can only be changed by deleting the row and reinserting it into a different table. If the self-referencing column is system generated, then deleting the row and reinserting it into a different table will result in the row having a different reference value. The contents of subtables are therefore always disjoint and cannot represent overlapping constraints.

To illustrate the behavior of rows in a typed table, consider the following insert statements over the Person hierarchy from the School Database Enterprise. Notice that since the student and faculty tables inherit attributes from the person table, the insert statements for these tables include values for the inherited attributes. The value for the self-referencing column is automatically generated as a result of the insert statements. For the purpose of this example, ignore the total specialization constraint on the person hierarchy.

```
insert into person  values ('PP111', 'Joe', 'Smith', '2/18/82');
insert into person  values ('PP222', 'Alice', 'Black', '2/15/80');
insert into student values ('ST333', 'Sue', 'Jones', '8/23/87', 'freshman');
insert into student values ('ST444', 'Joe', 'White', '5/16/86', 'sophomore');
insert into faculty  values ('FA555', 'Alice', 'Cooper', '9/2/51', 'professor');
```

A graphical view of the resulting rows is shown in Figure 3.4. This graphical view does *not* necessarily reflect the manner in which the tables are actually implemented, but it provides the simplest view for explaining the semantics of the hierarchy in response to select, insert, delete, and update statements.

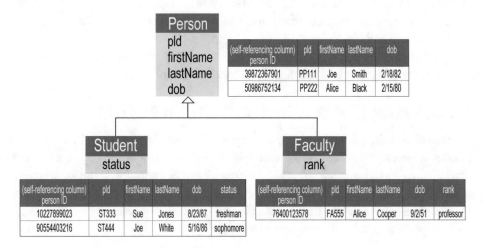

Figure 3.4: Rows in the Person Table Hierarchy

3.5.2   QUERYING A TABLE HIERARCHY

Subtable/supertable relationships in typed tables support the ISA constraint introduced in Chapter 1, meaning that an instance of a subtable is an instance of its supertable. As as result, consider the query below over the person table, where the double vertical bar (||) is the string concatenation operator.

```
select    firstName || '' || lastName
from      person;
```

The query result will produce the following names as output: 'Joe Smith', 'Alice Black', 'Sue Jones', 'Joe White', 'Alice Cooper'.

The query essentially performs the union of the person table with all of the common attributes from rows of the subtables to return all direct instances of the person table as well as all instances of its subtables. In contrast, consider the following query over the faculty table.

```
select      firstName || ' ' || lastName
from        faculty;
```

The only name returned from the query is 'Alice Cooper'. Unless otherwise specified, a query over any typed table will return the direct instances of the table as well as instances of its subtables and *not* instances of its supertables. A similar query over the **student** table will return 'Sue Jones' and 'Joe White'.

To retrieve only the direct instances of a table, the **only** option can be used in the **from** clause to constrain the query results. The following query will only return 'Joe Smith' and 'Alice Black' in the query result.

```
select      firstName || ' ' || lastName
from        only (person);
```

3.5.3   DELETING ROWS FROM A TABLE HIERARCHY

Consider the case of a **delete** statement expressed over the root of a table hierarchy. The following statement over the **person** table will delete any row from the table hierarchy with the first name of 'Alice', even if the most specific type of the row is a **student** or a **faculty**. This behavior is as expected according to the ISA constraint for class hierarchies since a **student ISA person** and a **faculty ISA person**. In particular, the statement will delete the rows for 'Alice Black' and 'Alice Cooper'.

```
delete from person where firstName = 'Alice';
```

Deleting a tuple from a subtable also implicitly deletes the tuple from its supertables. For example, since a **student ISA person**, the deletion of 'Sue Jones' from the **student** table will also result in 'Sue Jones' no longer being visible from the **person** table (i.e., because the tuple no longer exists in the **student** table).

```
delete from student where firstName = 'Sue' and lastName = 'Jones';
```

As a result of the above **delete** statement, a query to return all rows of the **person** table will not include 'Sue Jones' since the row for 'Sue Jones' has been removed from the table hierarchy. Recall that each row has a most specific type. Once the row is removed, it is considered to be removed from the entire table hierarchy.

It is possible to restrict the rows that are deleted using the **only** clause. The following statement will delete rows from **person** with a first name of 'Joe' only if the person does not have a most specific type of **student** or **faculty**. As a result of the statement, the row for 'Joe Smith' is the only row deleted. The row for 'Joe White' still remains in the table hierarchy.

```
delete from only (person) where firstName = 'Joe';
```

3.5.4   UPDATING ROWS IN A TABLE HIERARCHY

The **update** statement operates in a manner similar to the **delete** statement. For example, the following statement will change the first name of each row in the **person** table and in any subtables of person. As a result, the name of 'Sue Jones' in the student table will be changed even though the query is expressed over the person table.

```
update    person
set       firstName = 'Suzy'
where     firstName = 'Sue';
```

To restrict an update operation to rows that do not appear in any subtables, the only clause is used. The query below will change the first name of Joe Smith in the person table and not the first name of Joe White in the student table.

```
update    only (person)
set       firstName = 'Joey'
where     firstName = 'Joe';
```

It is important to note that the condition in the where clause of an update statement also applies to all rows that are in supertables of the table identified in the update statement. If the set clause refers to attributes that do not appear in the supertable, then the set clause is ignored.

3.5.5   CHECKPOINT: TYPED TABLE HIERARCHIES

Structured types together with typed tables can be used to provide the object-relational equivalent of classes in the object-oriented data model. Instances of typed tables have object identifiers that are known as references, where references can be system generated, user-defined, or based on attributes of the table. The use of the under clause in structured types and their corresponding table definitions can be used to form tables into hierarchies that support inheritance of state and behavior. Multiple inheritance is not supported in the formation of table hierarchies. Queries can be expressed over table hierarchies to return all of the objects in a table, including objects in the subtables. Queries can also be restricted to return only the direct instances of a table. As with object-oriented data models, overlapping subclasses, abstract classes, total specialization, and attributed-defined subclasses from conceptual models are not directly supported by table hierarchies in the SQL standard. Programmers must find creative ways to enforce such constraints over table hierarchies.

3.6   REFERENCE TYPES

Previous sections in this chapter have mentioned the use of the self-referencing column. Recall that the self-referencing column is the internal object identifier, or reference, to a row. This reference is a data type known as a *reference type*, or ref. The syntax for defining ref types is shown in Figure 3.5. A ref type is a valid SQL data type and can therefore be used to define the type of a column in a table, an attribute in a structured type definition, a variable, or a parameter. When used as an attribute of a structured type in combination with the use of typed tables, reference types can be used to model object associations between typed tables that are based on object identity rather than on foreign keys. Reference types therefore provide a way of modeling object relationships as in the object-oriented data model.

```
<reference type> ::= ref (<referenced_type>) [<scope_clause>] [array [unsigned_integer]] [<reference_scope_check>]
                    /* [ ] part of syntax*/

<scope_clause> ::= scope <table_name>

<referenced_type>::= <user_defined_type_name>

<reference_scope_check> ::= references are [not] checked [on delete <action>]
```

Figure 3.5: Syntax for Defining Reference Types

To illustrate the use of reference types, consider again the SCHOOL DATABASE ENTERPRISE in Figure 3.1. There is a 1:N relationship between CampusClub and Faculty, where a club has one advisor and a faculty member can advise many clubs. There is also a M:N relationship between CampusClub and Student, indicating that students are members of many clubs and clubs have many student members. The campusClubUdt type can be redefined to use reference types as a means for defining relationships with faculty and student objects.

```
    create type campusClubUdt as
    (  cId        varchar(10),
       name       varchar(50) not null,
       location   locationUdt,
       phone      varchar(12),
       advisor    ref(facultyUdt), /* Reference to a faculty object */
       members    ref(studentUdt) array[50]) /* References to student objects */
       instantiable not final ref is system generated;
    create table campusClub of campusClubUdt
    (  primary key (cId),
       ref is campusClubId system generated);
```

The revised campusClubUdt illustrates the use of two different ref types, one to model a single-valued relationship and another to model a multivalued relationship. The type of advisor is defined to be ref(facultyUdt). This type definition indicates that the value to be stored in the advisor attribute is the value of a self-referencing column from a typed table that is associated with the facultyUdt type, thus storing an object reference to a row instead of a value-oriented foreign key as in traditional relational tables. The name of the self-referencing column of the faculty table can be used to assign a ref value to a column defined as a ref type. In the update statement below, personID is the name of the self-referencing column from the definition of the faculty typed table (inherited from the person typed table).

```
    update campusClub
    set advisor =
    (  select      personID
       from        person
       where       firstName = 'Alice' and lastName = 'Cooper')
    where name = 'Campus Computer Club';
```

The members attribute in campusClubUdt is defined to be an array of references to student objects, defined as ref(studentUdt) array[50], thus allowing typed tables to directly model multivalued object references. Arrays of references are generally manipulated and queried through the use of SQL routines.

3.6.1   SCOPES AND REFERENCE CHECKING

Since a structured type can be used as the basis for creating several typed tables, a scope clause can be used in the specification of a ref type to restrict reference values to those from a specific typed table. The syntax for the scope clause is shown in Figure 3.5.

If the scope clause is omitted, then the reference value stored in the attribute can be a row from any table having the specified type. If the scope clause is specified, then a reference scope check can also be specified. Specifying that references are checked indicates that dangling references (i.e., invalid reference values) are not allowed. By default, references are not checked. The on delete clause of the reference scope check syntax allows the user to specify the same referential actions as used with the specification of referential integrity for foreign keys. In the example below, the advisor attribute is redefined to indicate that object references must be from the faculty table and that references are checked for validity. The on delete clause indicates that deletion of a referenced faculty object will cause the advisor attribute to be set to null.

```
    advisor ref(facultyUdt) scope faculty
        references are checked on delete set null;
```

Notice that the syntax in Figure 3.3 also supports the specification of table scopes and reference checks during the creation of typed tables. The syntax is the same as that used in the specification of structured types.

3.6.2   QUERYING REFERENCE TYPES

When querying tables that contain columns with reference values, users are generally not interested in seeing the reference value. The reference value is typically a system-generated value that is useful for establishing object relationships but has little meaning from the users point of view. Instead, the reference value is typically used to perform an *implicit join* as a means of accessing some attribute of the row that is being referenced.

The SQL standard supports the dereference operator, denoted as a right arrow, $\rightarrow$, to traverse through object references. The query below returns the name of the advisor of the Campus Computer

Club. The query is expressed over the campusClub table, but the value returned is from the faculty table. The dereference operator is used to implicitly join the campusClub and faculty tables based on the reference value. The dereference operator provides a more concise, object-oriented way of traversing from one object to another than the use of explicit join conditions over relational tables.

```
select     advisor → firstName
from       campusClub
where      name = 'Campus Computer Club';
```

The SQL standard also provides a deref() function than can be used to return the entire structured type that is associated with a reference value. The following query will return all instances of the facultyUdt type for advisors of campus clubs that are located in the Brickyard Building. The result of the query is a table with one column of type facultyUdt. The resulting table can then be queried to access any of the attributes of the advisors.

```
select     deref (advisor)
from       campusClub c
where      c.location.bldg = 'Brickyard Building';
```

The use of reference types is an important feature for mapping object-oriented conceptual designs to an object-relational representation. The following section provides more specific examples of the use of reference types in the mapping process.

3.7   MAPPING TO THE SQL STANDARD OBJECT-RELATIONAL FEATURES

This section describes how to map EER and UML conceptual designs to object-relational database designs. The techniques presented in this section build on the conceptual-to-relational mapping techniques that are summarized in Appendix A. The process of mapping classes, attributes, and associations is presented in the context of the Abstract Enterprise from Figure 1.1 (EER version) and from Figure 1.2 (UML version). These concepts are combined with mapping techniques for class hierarchies to present the complete object-relational representation of the SCHOOL DATABASE ENTERPRISE from Figure 3.1. The HOLLYWOOD ENTERPRISE in Figure 1.25 (EER version) and in Figure 1.26 (UML version) will also be used to illustrate mapping techniques for categories. As in Chapter 2, side-by-side EER and UML diagrams are used to illustrate the mappings. The reader should refer to Appendix A if necessary for a review of relational mapping issues in support of the object-relational techniques described in this section.

3.7.1   CLASSES, ATTRIBUTES, AND ASSOCIATIONS

The general approach to mapping EER and UML conceptual diagrams to object-relational features is to translate each class in the conceptual design to a structured type with a corresponding typed table and to represent associations between classes using reference types. Reference types can be combined with arrays to implement multivalued associations. Arrays and methods can also be used to implement multivalued attributes and derived attributes, respectively. The following subsections elaborate on the details of the mapping process.

3.7.1.1 Simple and Derived Attributes

Recall the class A of Figure 1.3 that has simple attributes (keyOfA, attrOfA), a composite attribute (compositeOfA) and a derived attribute (derivedAttr). Using the object-relational features of the SQL standard, class A is mapped to a typed table a with a corresponding structured type aUdt.

```
create type aUdt as
(   keyOfA          varchar(3),
    attrOfA         varchar(3),
    compositeOfA row(attrA1 varchar(3), attrA2 varchar(3), attrA3 varchar(3)))
    instantiable not final ref is system generated
    method derivedAttr() returns varchar(3);
create table a of aUdt
(   primary key(keyOfA),
    ref is aID system generated);
```

The simple attributes keyOfA and attrOfA are defined in the structured type as varchar, for simplicity. Since the SQL standard provides inherent support for complex types, the composite attribute of A can be directly represented as either a row type or a structured type. For simplicity, a row type is used in this example. Structured types are useful for representing composite attributes when the composite attribute must be used in multiple table or type definitions or when there is a need for defining parameters or variables that correspond to the composite value. Structured types are also useful for representing composite values that require specific method definitions for manipulation of the composite value.

The derived attribute derivedAttr is defined as a method within the aUdt structured type. Recall that a constructor function as well as observor and mutator functions will also be generated for keyOfA, attrOfA, and compositeOfA. Constraints associated with the attributes of the class are expressed in the typed table definition. The definition of a identifies keyOfA as the primary key of the typed table, in addition to the use of a system generated internal object identifier aID. Even with the use of object identifiers, primary keys are still useful from an application-oriented point-of-view.

3.7.1.2 Multivalued Attributes

The class C of Figure 1.4 illustrates a multivalued attribute, named multiValuedAttr. In a pure relational representation, a multivalued attribute must be mapped to its own table, including the key attribute of the class. Since the SQL standard supports arrays as a collection type, multiValuedAttr can be directly represented as an attribute of the structured type cUdt for the typed table c, where the attribute is defined as an array of a specific data type (varchar in this case).

```
create type cUdt as
(  keyOfC              varchar(3),
   attrOfC             varchar(3),
   multiValuedAttr   varchar(3) array[10])
   instantiable not final ref is system generated;
create table c of cUdt ...
```

3.7.1.3 Bidirectional Associations Without Attributes

In ODL as described in Chapter 2, bidirectional associations without attributes are mapped to a relationship with an inverse specification for both classes involved in the association. The object-relational features of the SQL standard do not support inverse specifications as in ODL, but reference types can be used on each side of the association to achieve an object-oriented approach to the representation of bidirectional associations. As an example, consider the 1:1 bc association between the classes B and C as illustrated in Figure 1.8. Define a typed table b having a structured type bUdt with an attribute named bTOc of type ref (cUdt). Also define a typed table c having a structured type cUdt with an attribute cTOb of type ref (bUdt).

```
create type bUdt as
( ...
   bTOc ref(cUdt) scope c references are checked on delete no action,
   ...)
   instantiable not final ref is system generated;
create type cUdt as
(...
   cTOb ref(bUdt) scope b references are checked on delete set null,
   ...)
   instantiable not final ref is system generated;
create table b of bUdt ... bTOc with options not null ...
create table c of cUdt ...
```

Note that this definition is a circular reference, which technically requires the use of an alter type statement to add the definition of bToC to the bUdt type after the cUdt type is defined. For conceptual presentation of the type definitions in this example and in other circular definitions in the remainder of this chapter, the alter type statement is omitted.

Unlike the object-oriented data model which provides automatic support for inverse relationships, the user is responsible for maintaining the inverse relationship that exists between b and c. For example, if the attribute bTOc for a row b_i in b is assigned the object reference for the row c_j in c, then the application must be designed to update the attribute cTOb of the row c_j to the object reference for the row b_i. The inverse relationship can be maintained through the use of triggers or stored procedures.

The cardinality ratio constraints of the association are inherent in the specification of the association by defining the reference type on each side of the association as a single-valued attribute.

For the bc association in Figure 1.8, the type of each association is a single object reference of the specified structured type. The total participation of class B in the bc association is defined by using the not null constraint in the typed table definition for b (note the different syntax for defining column constraints in typed tables as specified in Figure 3.3). In the object-oriented database mapping of Chapter 2, this constraint must be handled as part of the behavior of the object and is not directly supported by the database. The object-relational representation therefore provides more direct database support for the enforcement of attribute constraints.

Each reference in the bc association is constrained to store object references from a specific typed table using the scope clause. Even though object-relational implementations do not automatically maintain inverse relationships in bidirectional associations, the references are checked clause can be used to enforce referential integrity. As a result, the bTOc and cTOb attributes will never contain reference values for rows that do not exist in the referenced tables. If the clause is omitted or if the specification is references are not checked, then the attribute values may contain dangling reference values. In addition, an on delete action can be specified. For the bTOc attribute, the delete action is no action since rows of b have required participation in the association. As a result, a row in c cannot be deleted if it is related to a row in b since deleting a row in c may violate the total participation constraint of b. In the opposite direction, the action is set null, indicating that if a row in b is deleted, then the cTOb attribute can be set to null, thus reflecting the partial participation of c in the association.

The mapping approach described above for a 1:1 association also applies to a bidirectional association without attributes having 1:N or M:N cardinality ratios. The only difference is that the type on the many side of the association is an array of reference types. To illustrate the mapping, consider an M:N association between the classes B and C (not represented in the ABSTRACT ENTERPRISE). The bidirectional association is mapped to an object-relational schema using two separate arrays of reference types, where a row in b is related to potentially many object references to rows of c and a row of c is related to potentially many object references to rows of b.

```
create type bUdt as
(...
    bTOMANYc ref(cUdt) scope c array[10] references are checked
    on delete cascade,
    ...)
    instantiable not final ref is system generated;
create type cUdt as
(...
    cTOMANYb ref(bUdt) scope b array[10] references are checked
    on delete set null,
    ...)
    instantiable not final ref is system generated;
create table b of bUdt ...
create table c of cUdt ...
```

The example below illustrates the mapping for a 1:N association between B and C, where a row of b is related to potentially many object references to rows of c but a row of c is related to at most one object reference to a row of b.

```
create type bUdt as
(...
    bTOMANYc ref(cUdt) scope c array[10] references are checked
    on delete cascade,
    ...)
    instantiable not final ref is system generated;
create type cUdt as
(...
    cTOb ref(bUdt) scope b references are checked in delete set null,
    ...)
    instantiable not final ref is system generated;
create table b of bUdt ...
create table c of cUdt ...
```

3.7.1.4 Bidirectional Associations With Attributes

When binary associations have attributes, an association typed table must be introduced to represent the attributes of the association. The association table includes two attributes with reference types - one for the structured type of each typed table participating in the binary association. Consider the M:N ab association between classes A and B that has a descriptive attribute attrOfAB, as shown in Figure 1.6. Figure 2.2 gives the UML diagram for the corresponding reified association. An association table is defined as a typed table named ab with a structured type abUdt having the attribute attrOfAB and two reference type attributes: abTOa and abTOb. The reference type of abTOa is ref(aUdt) having scope a, indicating the row of typed table a that is participating in the relationship instance. Similarly, the reference type of abTOb is ref(bUdt) having scope b, indicating the row of typed table b that is participating in the relationship instance. The definitions for the structured types involved in the association include attributes with reference types to the structured type of the association table.

```
create type aUdt as
(...
    aTOab ref(abUdt) scope ab array[10] references are checked on delete set null,
    ...)
    instantiable not final ref is system generated;
create type bUdt as
(...
    bTOab ref(abUdt) scope ab array[10] references are checked on delete set null,
    ...)
    instantiable not final ref is system generated;
```

```
create type abUdt as
(. . .
    attrOfAB varchar(3),
    abTOa ref(aUdt) scope a references are checked on delete cascade,
    abTOb ref(bUdt) scope b references are checked on delete cascade
    . . .)
    instantiable not final ref is system generated;
create table a of aUdt . . .
create table b of bUdt . . .
create table ab of abUdt . . .
```

The structured type aUdt contains the attribute aTOab having as its type ref(abUdt) array[10], since an object of type aUdt is related to potentially many objects of type bUdt through the abUdt structured type of the ab association table (the number 10 in the array definition is arbitrary and can be set to a number appropriate for the specific association). Similarly, the structured type bUdt contains the attribute bTOab having as its type ref(abUdt) array[10], since an object of type bUdt is related to potentially many objects of type aUdt through the abUdt structured type of the ab association table. Since the participation of a in the association is required, the application will need to ensure that there is always at least one value in the aTOab array.

3.7.1.5   Recursive Associations

The mapping of recursive associations is similar to the mapping of non-recursive associations, except that the recursive association is relating the typed table to itself using a recursive reference to the structured type of the typed table. In Figure 1.9, the class B has a recursive association bb. A straightforward approach for mapping a recursive association is to use the role names of the association as the names of the reference attributes in the structured type. For example, the parent role of the bb association is of type ref(bUdt) having the child attribute as its implied inverse relationship. The child attribute is an array of references to bUdt, representing the children of the parent. As in non-recursive binary associations, the user is responsible in an object-relational implementation for maintaining the integrity of the relationship, although reference checks and delete actions can be specified to support maintenance of the association.

```
create type bUdt as
( . . .
    parent ref(bUdt) scope b references are checked on delete set null,
    child ref(bUdt) scope b array[10] references are checked on delete set null,
    . . .)
    instantiable not final ref is system generated;
create table b of bUdt . . .
```

3.7.1.6 N-ary Associations

The mapping of N-ary associations is similar to the mapping of binary associations having descriptive attributes. An association table is defined to represent the N-ary association, and there are N reference attributes defined, one for the structured type of each typed table involved in the association. Consider as an example, the ternary relationship given in Figure 1.10. In this relationship, finance is the association table having the structured type financeUdt with reference attributes financedBank, financedCar, and financedPerson that, respectively, refer to the bank, car, and person involved in the transaction. In the inverse direction, the structured types bankUdt, carUdt, and personUdt define reference attributes that point back to the financeUdt structured type. The cardinality of each attribute indicates the number of times a row from the typed table can participate in a finance association. The attributes in bankUdt and personUdt, for example, are defined as arrays, indicating that a bank can finance many cars and a person can buy many cars. The attribute in carUdt is single-valued, indicating that a car can only be sold once.

```
    create type financeUdt
    ( ...
        financedBank       ref(bankUdt) scope bank
                           references are checked on delete cascade,
        financedCar        ref(carUdt) scope car
                           references are checked on delete cascade,
        financedPerson     ref(personUdt) scope person
                           references are checked on delete cascade,
        ...)
    instantiable not final ref is system generated;
    create type bankUdt /* inverse of financedBank */
    ( ...
        carsFinanced       ref(financedUdt) scope finance array[10]
                           references are checked on delete set null,
        ...)
    instantiable not final ref is system generated;
    create type carUdt /* inverse of financedCar */
    ( ...
        financedBy         ref(financeUdt) scope finance
                           references are checked on delete set null,
        ...)
    instantiable not final ref is system generated;
    create type personUdt /* inverse of financedPerson */
    ( ...
        carsFinanced       ref(financeUdt) scope finance array[10]
                           references are checked on delete set null,
        ...)
    instantiable not final ref is system generated;
```

```
create table finance of financeUdt . . .
create table bank of bankUdt . . .
create table car of carUdt . . .
create table person of personUdt . . .
```

3.7.1.7 Unidirectional Associations

UML conceptual class diagrams have the ability to represent unidirectional associations through navigability. A unidirectional association stores the association in one direction. To specify a unidirectional association, define a reference attribute within the structured type of one side of the association. For example, the unidirectional association bc shown in Figure 1.12 is defined as a reference attribute in the structured type bUdt having the type ref(cUdt). The inverse of the unidirectional association is derived by providing a method in cUdt to derive the bUdt reference to which an instance of cUdt is related.

```
create type bUdt
( . . .
   bTOc ref(cUdt) scope c references are checked on delete no action,
   . . . )
   instantiable not final ref is system generated;
create type cUdt ( . . . )
   instantiable not final ref is system generated
   method cTOb( ) return bUdt;
create table b of bUdt . . . bTOc with options not null . . .
create table c of cUdt . . .
```

3.7.1.8 Weak Entities

A weak entity of an EER diagram is typically related to its identifying owner by a 1:N relationship. In Figure 1.13, the Weak class is related to its identifying owner class A by its identifying relationship dependsOn. The candidate key of a weak entity is formed by the combination of the primary key of its identifying owner and its own partial key, which uniquely identifies the weak object in the context of the identifying owner. In the UML diagram of Figure 1.13, dependsOn is represented as a qualified association based on the partialKey.

To map this type of association to an object-relational representation, create a typed table for the weak entity with a composite key that includes the key of the typed table for the owner class. The structured type for the typed table of the weak class can also include a reference attribute to the row of the typed table that represents the owner class.

```
create type aUdt as
( . . .
   keyOfA        varchar(3),
   linkToWeak    ref(weakUdt) scope weak array[10]
                 references are checked on delete set null,
```

```
    ... )
      instantiable not final ref is system generated;
   create type weakUdt as
   ( ...
      partialKey      varchar(3),
      keyOfA          varchar(3),
      linkToOwner    ref(aUdt) scope a references are checked on delete cascade,
      ... )
      instantiable not final ref is system generated;
   create table a of aUdt
   (   primary key (keyOfA) ... );
   create table weak of weakUdt
   (   linkToOwner with options not null,
       foreign key(partialKey) references a(keyOfA) on delete cascade,
       primary key(partialKey, keyOfA) ... );
```

For the semantics expressed in Figure 1.13, the reference attribute linkToWeak defined in aUdt represents the array of weakUdt objects associated with an instance of aUdt. The inverse association defined as linkToOwner in weakUdt links an instance of weakUdt to its identifying aUdt owner instance. The a typed table defines the attribute keyOfA as its primary key. In addition, the weak typed table includes the key of the identifying owner (keyOfA) in combination with the partialKey to create a composite key for the weak table.

3.7.1.9   Constraints on Classes, Attributes, and Associations

When mapping the object-oriented conceptual data models to the relational data model, relevant implementation-level constraints to consider for classes, attributes, and associations include the specification of candidate keys, referential integrity, participation, and multiplicity constraints. Mapping to the object-relational features of the SQL standard can still make use of primary key and uniqueness constraints to specify candidate keys. The referential integrity constraint is also extended to the specification of reference types to make sure that the value of a reference attribute refers to an object identifier in the referenced table. In addition, the scope clause can be used to restrict the reference to be from a specific typed table. The reference type specification in the SQL standard also inherently supports simple cardinality constraints, where arrays can be used with reference types to represent multivalued associations. A total participation constraint is inherently supported by placing a not null constraint on a reference attribute. When a total participation constraint is used together with a multivalued association, the application may need to ensure that an array of references always contains at least one value. Specific upper and lower bounds in multivalued associations must also be enforced by the application. Such constraints can be coded into the behavioral aspects of the structured type definition.

In comparison to object-oriented databases, the representation of bidirectional associations in an object-relational schema using references types does not automatically support the specification and maintenance of inverse relationships. The maintenance of inverse relationships must be coded into the behavior of the application.

3.7.2 CHECKPOINT: OBJECT-RELATIONAL MAPPING OF CLASSES, ATTRIBUTES, AND ASSOCIATIONS

Table 3.2 summarizes the mapping of classes, attributes, and associations to the object-relational features of the SQL standard using names such as cUdt and sUdt to represent generic type definitions. The first column indicates the component being mapped. The second column indicates the corresponding type to be defined in the schema. The third column gives either the type and table definitions associated with the type or the attribute definition that is added to the definition of the type to realize the component of the object model. The mapping summary assumes the use of bidirectional associations. Remember that structured types associated with typed tables must be defined as instantiable and as not final. The specification for generating object references must be consistent between the structured type and the typed table (e.g., system generated in both the structured type and the corresponding typed table). Standard column and table constraints can be defined on the attributes of a structured type in the typed table definition.

Table 3.2: Summary of Object Relational Mapping Heuristics for Classes, Attributes, and Associations.

Component	Type	Object-Relational Definition
class C	cUdt	create type cUdt as (...); create table c of cUdt (...);
single-valued attribute s of C	cUdt	s typeOfS
composite attribute s of C (implemented as a row type)	cUdt	s row(...)
composite attribute s of C (implemented as a structured type)	sUdt cUdt	create type sUdt as (...); s sUdt
multivalued attribute m of C	cUdt	m typeOfM array[n]
binary association, no attributes (1:1 shown)	c1Udt c2Udt	c1TOc2 ref(c2Udt) scope c2 c2TOc1 ref(c1Udt) scope c1
binary association ac with attributes (e.g., attrOfAc) Use an association class (M:N shown)	c1Udt c2Udt acUdt	c1TOac ref(acUdt) scope ac array[n] c2TOac ref(acUdt) scope ac array[n] attrOfAC typeOfattrOfAC, acTOc1 ref(c1Udt) scope c1, acTOc2 ref(c2Udt) scope c2
recursive association c (1:N shown)	cUdt	parent ref(cUdt) scope c, child ref(cUdt) scope c array[n]

Figure 3.6 presents the complete object-relational schema for the unidirectional version of the ABSTRACT ENTERPRISE in Figure 1.12. The specification of the schema is more complex than

```
create type aUdt as
( keyOfA          varchar(3),
  attrOfA         varchar(3),
  compositeOfA    row (attrA1 varchar(3), attrA2 varchar(3), attrA3 varchar(3)),
  aTOab           ref(abUdt) scope ab array[10] references are checked on delete set null,
  aTOb            ref(bUdt) scope ab references are checked on delete cascade,
  attrOfBA        varchar(3),
  linkToWeak      ref(weakUdt) scope weak array[10] references are checked on delete set null)
  instantiable not final ref is system generated
  method derivedAttr() returns varchar(3);

create table a of aUdt
( aTOb with options not null,
  aTOab with options not null,
  primary key(keyOfA),
  ref is aID system generated);

create type weakUdt as
( partial Key     varchar(3),
  keyOfA          varchar(3),
  attrOfWk        varchar(3),
  linkToOwner     ref(aUdt) scope a references are checked on delete cascade)
  instantiable not final ref is system generated;

create table weak of weakUdt
( linkToOwner with options not null,
  primary key(partialKey, keyOfA),
  foreign key(partialKey) references a(keyOfA) on delete cascade,
  ref is wID system generated);

create type bUdt as
( keyOfB          varchar(3),
  attrOfB         varchar(3),
  parent          ref(bUdt) scope b references are checked on delete set null,
  bTOab           ref(abUdt) scope ab array[10] references are checked on delete set null,
  bTOc            ref(cUdt) scope c references are checked on delete cascade)
  instantiable not final ref is system generated
  method bTOa() returns aUdt,
  method children() returns bUdt array[10];

create table b of bUdt
( bTOc with options not null,
  primary key(keyOfB),
  ref is bID system generated);
```

Figure 3.6: The SQL Standard Object-Relational Schema of the Unidirectional ABSTRACT ENTERPRISE (*Continues.*)

```
create type abUdt as .
( attrOfAB          varchar(3),
  abTOa             ref(aUdt) scope a references are checked on delete cascade,
  abTOb             ref(bUdt) scope b references are checked on delete cascade)
  instantiable not final ref is system generated;

create table ab of abUdt
( abTOa with options not null,
  abTOb with options not null,
  ref is abID system generated);

create type cUdt as
( keyOfC            varchar(3),
  attrOfC           varchar(3),
  multiValuedAttr   varchar(3) array[10])
  instantiable not final ref is system generated
  method cTOb() returns bUdt;

create table c of cUdt
( primary key(keyOfC),
  ref is cID system generated);
```

Figure 3.6: (*Continued.*) The SQL Standard Object-Relational Schema of the Unidirectional AB-STRACT ENTERPRISE

the pure relational version in Figure A.2 of Appendix A. The object-relational version, however, supports the direct representation of multivalued attributes and the use of reference types together with arrays to represent 1:1, 1:N, and M:N associations between classes, where associations are based on object references rather than foreign keys. Arrays of references must be manipulated and queried through the use of SQL routines. Unlike the object-oriented mapping in Chapter 2, the user must maintain inverse relationships. The unidirectional mapping in Figure 3.6, however, illustrates how unidirectional relationships can be used to directly represent the relationship in one direction and to derive the relationship in the opposite direction through the use of a method (see the method definitions in cUdt and in bUdt that correspond to the inverse of each unidirectional relationship).

3.7.3   CLASS HIERARCHIES

The object-relational features of the SQL standard provide inherent support for the specification of class hierarchies. The inheritance of state and behavior is supported by the under clause in the structured type and typed table specifications. An example was provided in Section 3.3 using the Person hierarchy from the SCHOOL DATABASE ENTERPRISE.

The EER and UML conceptual data models both provide support for the specification of specialization constraints: disjoint versus overlapping specialization, and total or mandatory participation in the class specialization. The object-relational model of the SQL standard does not provide for an overlapping specialization of subclasses. Therefore, by default, a specialization in an object-relational schema is disjoint. As in most object-oriented database implementations, if an overlapping specialization is required for the application, the programmer must simulate the inheritance for all but one of the subtables by using an explicit reference from the overlapping subtables to the supertable and explicitly calling the methods of the supertable to which it is related. The object will, of course, have multiple identifiers, one for each typed table (simulating the overlapping subtables) to which it belongs, and inheritance from the supertable to the overlapping subtables will not be inherently supported. The implementation of the overlapping specialization constraint therefore requires more coding effort on the part of the programmer to correctly represent the semantics of an overlapping specialization. The relational mapping techniques described in Appendix A can be used to simulate overlapping specialization.

The total specialization constraint is supported in the SQL standard for hierarchies of structured types but not for hierarchies of typed tables. In a structured type hierarchy, the supertype can be defined as not instantiable, while the subtypes can be defined as instantiable. The supertype therefore becomes an abstract type where the type can only be instantiated at the subtype level. But when structured types are used together with typed table hierarchies, structured types must be defined as instantiable. The total specialization constraint must therefore be enforced through the application code by only allowing the insertion of objects at the subtable level.

The object-relational features of the SQL standard do not support the specification of shared subclasses from the EER model or the concept of interface classes from UML class diagrams. Attribute-defined subclasses from the EER model and discriminators from UML are also not inherently supported. If such features are used in a conceptual model that must be mapped to an object-relational implementation, the programmer must find creative solutions to the implementation of such requirements.

3.7.4   CATEGORIES

A category in the EER or the Xor constraint in UML can be represented by introducing a typed table for the category. Attributes are introduced in the structured type of the category typed table to represent the association to its related superclasses.

The standard example of a category that has been used in previous chapters is the partial Sponsor category from the HOLLYWOOD ENTERPRISE, where a Sponsor is either a Person or a Company, but a Person or a Company is not required to be a Sponsor. A unidirectional reference attribute is defined in the structured type sponsorUdt for each class participating in the category: personSponsor with a reference type of personUdt and companySponsor with a reference type of companyUdt. Only one of the unidirectional attributes can have a value at any given time. The other unidirectional attribute must always be null, since an instance of sponsorUdt cannot be related to both a personUdt and a companyUdt. This category constraint must be implemented within the behavior of sponsorUdt.

```
create type personUdt as ( ... )
   instantiable not final ref is system generated;
create type companyUdt as ( ... )
   instantiable not final ref is system generated;
create type sponsorUdt as
( ...
   personSponsor ref(personUdt),      //Can also be implemented as bidirectional
   companySponsor ref(companyUdt) //relationships for total categories.
   ... )
   instantiable not final ref is system generated;
create table person of personUdt ...
create table company of companyUdt ...
create table sponsor of sponsorUdt ...
```

When the category is partial, a unidirectional association is preferred. It is still possible to find out whether a person or company is a sponsor and to find the projects that they sponsor by navigating the unidirectional associations from the sponsor typed table. If the category is total, requiring that every person and every company must participate in the category, then the category associations can be implemented using bidirectional relationships, where personUdt and companyUdt contain reference attributes that point back to sponsorUdt. The use of bidirectional relationships provides an explicit access path from person and company to the sponsor category table. The total categorization constraint can be enforced in the person and company tables by defining the reference attribute to sponsorUdt to be not null. Again, the person category table must still enforce the exclusive-or constraint of the category.

3.8   CHECKPOINT

Figure 3.7 presents the complete SQL schema for the SCHOOL DATABASE ENTERPRISE in Figure 3.1. The schema uses the object-relational features of the standard to represent hierarchies and object associations. Whereas the clubs, advises, and chair associations from Figure 3.1 are implemented using bidirectional reference attributes between structured types, the associations for major and worksIn are implemented as unidirectional reference attributes with methods in departmentUdt to derive the inverse values. The mandatory participation constraint on the person hierarchy must be enforced through the application code that controls the insertion of rows into the student and faculty tables (not allowing direct insertion into the person table).

3.9   ORACLE: OBJECT-RELATIONAL DATABASE MAPPINGS

This section presents an object-relational version of the SCHOOL DATABASE ENTERPRISE implemented using Oracle 11g. The implementation illustrates the use of user-defined types, reference types, and typed tables, as well as Oracle's support for collections in the form of variable-sized arrays

```
create type personUdt as
( pId            varchar(11),
  firstName      varchar(20),
  lastName       varchar(20),
  dob            date)
  instantiable not final ref is system generated;

create type facultyUdt under personUdt as
( rank           varchar(10),
  advisorOf      ref(campusClubUdt) scope campusClub array[5]
                 references are checked on delete set null,
  worksIn        ref(departmentUdt) scope department
                 references are checked on delete no action,
  chairOf        ref(departmentUdt) scope department
                 references are checked on delete set null)
  instantiable not final;

create type studentUdt under personUdt as
( status         varchar(10),
  memberOf       ref(campusClubUdt) scope campusClub array[5]
                 references are checked on delete set null,
  major          ref(departmentUdt) scope department
                 references are checked on delete no action)
  instantiable not final;

create table person of personUdt
( primary key(pId),
  ref is personID system generated);
create table faculty of facultyUdt under person;
create table student of studentUdt under person;

create type departmentUdt as
 ( code          varchar(3),
  name           varchar(40),
  deptChair      ref(facultyUdt) scope faculty
                 references are checked on delete no action)
  instantiable not final ref is system generated
  method getStudents() returns studentUdt array[1000],
  method getFaculty() returns facultyUdt array[50];
```

Figure 3.7: The SQL Standard Object-Relational Schema of the School Database Enterprise. ©ACM, 2003. This is a minor revision of the work published in "Using UML Class Diagrams for a Comparative Analysis of Relational, Object-Oriented, and Object-Relational Database Mappings," by S. Urban and S. Dietrich in *Proceedings of the 34th ACM SIGCSE Technical Symposium on Computer Science Education,* (2003) http://doi.acm.org/10.1145/620000.611923 (*Continues.*)

```
create table department of departmentUdt
( primary key (code),
    deptChair with options not null,
    ref is departmentID system generated);

create type locationUdt as
( street          varchar(30),
  bldg            varchar(5),
  room            varchar(5)) not final;

create type campusClubUdt as
( cId             varchar(10),
  name            varchar(50),
  location        locationUdt,
  phone           varchar(12),
  advisor         ref(facultyUdt) scope faculty
                  references are checked on delete cascade,
  members         ref(studentUdt) scope student array[50]
                  references are checked on delete set null)
  instantiable not final ref is system generated;

create table campusClub of campusClubUdt
( primary key(cId),
  ref is campusClubID system generated);
```

Figure 3.7: (*Continued.*) The SQL Standard Object-Relational Schema of the SCHOOL DATABASE ENTERPRISE. ©ACM, 2003. This is a minor revision of the work published in "Using UML Class Diagrams for a Comparative Analysis of Relational, Object-Oriented, and Object-Relational Database Mappings," by S. Urban and S. Dietrich in *Proceedings of the 34th ACM SIGCSE Technical Symposium on Computer Science Education*, (2003) http://doi.acm.org/10.1145/620000.611923

(varrays) and nested tables, which is a feature that is not supported by the SQL standard. Object type hierarchies and a feature known as substitutable tables are used as a means to support class hierarchies.

Figure 3.8 shows a modified UML diagram of the SCHOOL DATABASE ENTERPRISE, with annotations that explain the manner in which relationships of the enterprise are mapped to the Oracle object features. The Person, CampusClub, and Department classes are translated into object types. The Student and Faculty classes are translated into subtypes under the type for the Person class to form a type hierarchy. Tables are then created for the types associated with the Person, CampusClub, and Department classes, where the table for the Person class is a substitutable table that holds all objects from the person type hierarchy.

The clubs association is implemented as a bidirectional association, with a varray of references on one side of the association and a nested table of references on the other side of the association for an object-oriented approach to the implementation of M:N associations. The getClubs method has been added to the Student class to provide a way to return the names of the clubs (rather than the references) in which a student participates. The 1:N advises association, also bidirectional, is implemented as a varray in Faculty to store a collection of references to the campus clubs that a faculty member advises. The getClubsAdvised method has been added to Faculty to return the names of the advised clubs. In CampusClub, an inverse reference attribute is used to point back to the advisor of the club. The chair association is also bidirectional, implemented as a reference attribute on each side of the relationship. The majorsIn and worksIn associations are unidirectional, with a reference attribute in Student and Faculty, respectively. The getStudents and getFaculty methods in Department are used to derive the inverse of each association. All of the relevant type and table definitions for the Oracle object-relational representation of Figure 3.8 appear in Figure 3.9.

3.9.1   OBJECT TYPES AND TYPE HIERARCHIES

In conformance with the SQL standard, Oracle supports the basic object-relational feature of object types. An object type is a composite structure that can have a set of attributes and methods. Below is a simple example of a person_t object type definition for the Person class without methods. Notice that the Oracle definition of an object type does not require the instantiation, finality, and reference generation clauses as in the SQL standard.

```
create or replace type person_t as object
(  pId          varchar2(9),
   firstName    varchar2(20),
   lastName     varchar2(20),
   dob          date);
```

To assign values to an object type, a variable can be created having the type of the object type. The following example illustrates how to assign values into the attributes of the person_t object type in PL/SQL.

```
declare
p  person_t;
begin
   p.pId := 'PR123456789';
   p.firstName := 'Terrence';
   p.lastName := 'Grand';
   p.dob := '10-NOV-1975';
end;
```

Oracle does not support row types from the SQL standard. When an object type is used as the attribute value of another object type, the attribute value is referred to as an *embedded object*. Embedded objects do not have object identifiers, but provide a way to define an attribute as containing a composite value. In the following example, the location attribute of the campusClub_t object type is used as an embedded object.

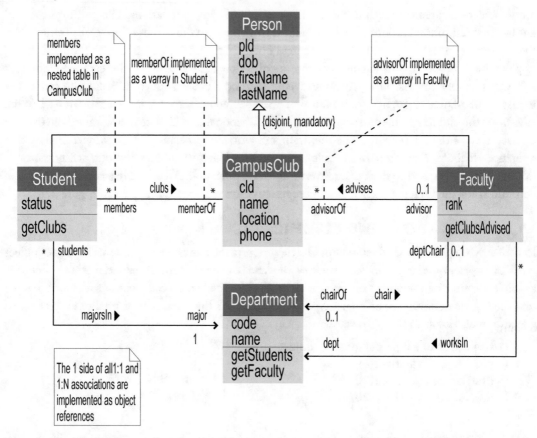

Figure 3.8: UML for the Oracle Object-Relational Case Study of the SCHOOL DATABASE ENTER-PRISE. ©ACM, 2003. This is a minor revision of the work published in "Using UML Class Diagrams for a Comparative Analysis of Relational, Object-Oriented, and Object-Relational Database Mappings," by S. Urban and S. Dietrich in *Proceedings of the 34th ACM SIGCSE Technical Symposium on Computer Science Education*, (2003) http://doi.acm.org/10.1145/620000.611923

```
create or replace type location_t as object
(  street    varchar2(30),
   bldg      varchar2(5),
   room      varchar2(5));
create or replace type campusClub_t as object
(  cId       number,
   name      varchar2(50),
   phone     varchar2(25),
   location  location_t,
   ... );
```

```
create or replace campusClub_t;
create or replace type campusClub_array as varray(50) of ref campusClub_t;

create or replace type string_array as varray(50) of varchar2(50);

create or replace type location_t as object
( street          varchar2(30),
  bldg            varchar2(5),
  room            varchar2(5));

create or replace type person_t as object
( pld             varchar2(9),
  firstName       varchar2(20),
  lastName        varchar2(20),
  dob             date)
  not final;

create or replace type department_t;

create or replace type student_t under person_t
( status          varchar2(10),
  major           ref department_t,    --relation major
  memberOf        campusClub_array,  --relation memberOf
  member function getClubs return string_array,
  pragma restrict_references (default, wnds, wnps))
  final;

create or replace type faculty_t under person_t
( rank            varchar2(25),
  advisorOf       campusClub_array, --relation advisorOf
  worksIn         ref department_t,    --relation worksIn
  chairOf         ref department_t,
  member function getClubsAdvised return string_array,
  pragma restrict_references(default, wnds, wnps))
  final;

create table person of person_t
( pld             primary key,
  firstName       not null,
  lastName        not null,
  dob             not null)
  object id system generated;

create or replace type student_array as varray(50) of ref student_t;
```

Figure 3.9: Oracle DDL for the SCHOOL DATABASE ENTERPRISE of the Object-Relational Mapping (*Continues.*)

```
create or replace type faculty_array as varray(50) of ref faculty_t;

create or replace type department_t as object
( code             varchar2(3),
  name             varchar2(40),
  deptChair        ref faculty_t,
  member function getStudents return student_array,
  member function getFaculty return faculty_array,
  pragma restrict_references(default, wnds, wnps));

create table department of department_t
( code             primary key,
  name             not null,
  constraint department_chair
  foreign key(deptChair) references person on delete set null)
  object id system generated;

create or replace type student_ntable as table of ref student_t;

create or replace type campusClub_t as object
( cld              number,
  name             varchar2(50),
  phone            varchar2(25),
  location         location_t,
  advisor          ref faculty_t,      --relation advised by
  members          student_ntable,     --relation member of
  constraint club_advisor
  foreign key (advisor) references person on delete set null,
  member function isAssociatedMember
          (candidate_member in ref student_t) return boolean,
  member function isAssociatedAdvisor
          (candidate_advisor in ref faculty_t) return boolean,
  pragma restrict_references(default, wnds, wnps));

create table campusClub of campusClub_t
( cld              primary key,
  name             not null)
  object id system generated
  nested table members store as club_members;

alter table club_members add(
  scope of (column_value) is person);

create unique index club_members_idx on
  club_members(nested_table_id, column_value);
```

Figure 3.9: (*Continued.*) Oracle DDL for the SCHOOL DATABASE ENTERPRISE of the Object-Relational Mapping.

When an object type is used as the type of a column in a traditional relational table, the value is referred to as a *column object*. Embedded and column objects are accessed and manipulated in the same way as described in the SQL standard for structured types. For example, consider the following table definition with a column object loc.

```
create table courseOffering(code int, loc location_t);
```

Data can be inserted into the table using the type constructor for location_t.

```
insert into courseOffering values (123, location_t('Orange Mall', 'CPCOM', '207'));
```

Object type definitions may also contain method specifications. The methods of an object type are functions or procedures that model the behavior of objects. Recall that methods in the SQL standard are limited to functions only. As in the SQL standard, the self parameter is an instance of the object type on which a method is invoked. The following example illustrates the PL/SQL code definition of the isAssociatedAdvisor function, where the declaration of the function is shown in the campusClub_t object type definition in Figure 3.9.

```
create or replace type body campusClub_t is
...
member function isAssociatedAdvisor (candidate_advisor in ref faculty_t)
    return boolean is
begin
    return (self.advisor = candidate_advisor);
end isAssociatedAdvisor;
end;
```

The isAssociatedAdvisor function determines whether a faculty member is an advisor of a club. Methods are implemented in the object type body definition for campusClub_t.

The declaration of the isAssociatedAdvisor function as well as the isAssociatedMember function in campusClub_t of Figure 3.9 is also accompanied by a pragma declaration. Pragmas are compiler directives. Pragmas do not affect the meaning of a program. They simply convey information to the compiler. Pragma restrict_references is used to control side effects in a function, asserting that a function does not read/write any database tables and/or package variables. The syntax is: pragma restrict_references (function_name, option [, option]). The function name of default can be used to specify that the pragma applies to all functions in the type definition. The pragma options are the following:

wnds – Writes no database state (does not modify database tables).

rnds – Reads no database state (does not query database tables).

wnps – Writes no package state (does not change the values of package variables).

rnps – Reads no package state (does not reference the values of package variables).

In addition to the methods explicitly defined in an object type definition, every object type has a system-defined constructor method, which is a method that creates a new instance of an object type and sets up the values of its attributes. The name of the constructor method is the name of the object type. Its parameters have the names and types of the object type's attributes. The constructor method is a function that returns an instance of an object type as its value. For example, the following invocation of the person_t constructor method returns an instance of the person_t object type with the specified attribute values. Unlike the definition of constructor methods in the SQL standard, the built-in constructor for an object type in Oracle accepts parameter values for the attributes of the type.

person_t('PR123456789', 'Terrence', 'Grand', '10-NOV-1975')

As in the SQL standard, Oracle enhances object features by supporting type inheritance. The user can create an object type as a supertype and form a type hierarchy by defining one or more subtypes of the supertype. As shown in Figure 3.9, student_t and faculty_t are defined as subtypes under person_t. Objects of type student_t, for example, will then inherit the attributes of person_t and also define additional attributes (status, major, and memberOf) and methods (getClubs) for objects of type student_t. As a supertype, person_t must be defined as not final so that subtypes can be defined. Unlike the SQL standard, a type at the bottom of the type hierarchy can be specified as final.

3.9.2 OBJECT TABLES

An object table is a table in which each row represents an object, where each object has a unique object identifier (OID). Objects that occupy complete rows in object tables are called *row objects*. Oracle allows row objects to be referenced, meaning that other row objects or relational rows may reference a row object using its OID.

The unique OID value can be specified using table constraints as either system-generated or based on the row object's primary key. The default OID value is system generated. Figure 3.9 shows how to create an object table based on an object type for the Person, CampusClub, and Department classes in the SCHOOL DATABASE ENTERPRISE, where the syntax is similar to that for defining object tables in the SQL standard. For example, object table person is defined based on the object type person_t. The ref is clause of the SQL standard is replaced by the object id clause to specify how object identifiers are generated. In Figure 3.9, all of the table definitions indicate that object identifiers are system generated. As in the standard, table and column constraints can be defined in the specification of the object table.

As a deviation from the SQL standard, object tables in Oracle cannot be formed into table hierarchies. Instead, Oracle supports the concept of substitutable tables. A substitutable table is a table that is capable of storing multiple object types from a type hierarchy. A substitutable table therefore has the polymorphic capability to store an object of a supertype and any subtype that can be substituted for the supertype. In Figure 3.9, the person table is a substitutable table since it is associated with the supertype of a type hierarchy. The person table is capable of storing objects of type person_t as well as objects of type student_t. Row objects are inserted as shown in the statements below, where each insert statement indicates the specific type of the object and includes values for attributes of person_t as well as values for the attributes of the subtype.

```
insert into person_table
    values (person_t('101','Sue','Jones','05/16/1955'));

insert into person_table
    values (student_t('102','Jim','Duncan','03/12/1989','senior',get _dref('CSE'),null);

insert into person_table
    values (faculty_t('103','Joe', 'Smith','10/21/1960','Professor',null,get_dref('CSE'),null);
```

The insert statements for objects of type student_t and faculty_t invoke the get_dref function, which is passed the name of a department and returns a reference to the associated department object. Reference types are addressed in the following subsection.

3.9.3   REFERENCE TYPES

Oracle supports reference types (refs) as defined in the SQL standard, where reference types can be used to define object-to-object relationships. In Oracle, a ref is a logical pointer to a row object. For example, in Figure 3.9, the advisor attribute of the campusClub_t object type refers to the object type faculty_t. Also in Figure 3.9, a ref type is used to model the major relationship between student_t and department_t.

3.9.3.1 Constraining Reference Types

A ref column or attribute can be constrained using a scope clause or a referential constraint clause. When a ref column is unconstrained, it may store object references to row objects contained in any object table of the corresponding object type. Unconstrained references may also lead to dangling references. Currently, Oracle does not permit storing object references that contain a primary-key based object identifier in unconstrained ref columns.

A ref column may be constrained in Oracle with a referential constraint similar to the specification for foreign keys. The deptChair column of the department table in Figure 3.9 illustrates the use of the references clause to specify a column referential constraint on deptChair. The clause specifies that a ref stored in a deptChair column must point to a valid row object in the person object table. This clause also implicitly restricts the scope of deptChair to the person object table.

A ref column may also be constrained by being scoped to a specific object table, using a scope clause as defined in the standard. The scope constraint is different from the referential constraint because the scope constraint has no implications on the referenced object (i.e., deleting a referenced object can still cause a dangling reference). The advisor column of the campusClub object table is constrained in Figure 3.9 using a references clause. The following alter table statement illustrates the use of the scope clause to alternatively constrain the advisor column to refer to objects in the person table.

```
alter table campusClub add (scope for (advisor) is person);
```

The unique and primary key constraints cannot be specified for ref columns. However, a unique index may be created on a scoped ref column to ensure the uniqueness of the ref values.

3.9.3.2   Using Reference Types

Queries involving objects make a distinction between row objects, refs, and object types. Oracle provides three functions to support queries involving objects:

- ref() is a function that takes a row object as its argument and returns the ref to that object.

- value() is a function that takes a row object and returns the instance of the object type.

- deref() is a function that takes a ref to an object and returns the instance of the object type.

As an example, consider the campusClub_t object type and its corresponding campusClub object table together with the following sequence of code:

```
declare
    club_ref   ref campusClub_t;
    club       campusClub_t;
    club_adv   faculty_t;
begin
    select     value(c), ref(c), deref(c.advisor) into club, club_ref, club_adv
    from       campusClub c
    where      c.name='The Hiking Club';
end;
```

In a select statement such as the one shown in the above code sequence, the table alias (c in this case) always contains a row object. To see the values of the attributes of the row object as defined in the object type, use value(c). To get the ref to the row object, use ref(c). To get values of the attributes of the object type associated with a ref, use the deref() function. The only difference between value and deref is the input to each function, where value takes a row object as input and deref takes a ref as input. In both cases, the output is the instance of the object type (i.e., a tuple of attribute values) associated with the object.

After executing the above query, club will contain a campusClub_t object type instance, club_ref will contain the ref of the object, and club_adv will contain an instance of the faculty_t object type. Recall that c.advisor is a ref to faculty_t. The deref function is therefore applied to a ref value to return the object type instance of the ref.

Recall that the insert statements for the person table invoked the get_dref function to retrieve the ref to a specific department object. The get_dref function is shown below, where the select statement retrieves a department object using the code attribute and returns the reference to the object for assignment to an attribute that is defined to be of type ref department_t.

```
create or replace function get_dref(d_code in varchar2)
    return ref department_t is
    d_ref ref department_t;
    cursor cr is
        select ref(d) from department d where d.code = d_code;
begin
    open cr; fetch cr into d_ref; close cr; return d_ref;
end get_dref;
```

Reference types can also be used in queries to construct path expressions as in object-oriented database queries. The query below returns a string value representing the name of the department in which the advisor of the Campus Computer Club works. The expression c.advisor.worksIn.name is a path expression, representing implicit joins between the object tables involved.

```
select    c.advisor.worksIn.name
from      campusClub c
where     c.name = 'Campus Computer Club';
```

3.9.4   QUERYING SUBSTITUTABLE TABLES

Since a substitutable table contains a heterogeneous collection of objects from a type hierarchy, queries over the table may need to indicate the specific types of objects to be returned. The following select statement will return information about all objects in the person table:

```
select    value(p)
from      person_table p;
```

To retrieve details only about objects that are subtypes of the declared type of the table, the is of clause can be used. The query below will only return objects of type student_t from the person table.

```
select    value(p)
from      person_table p
where     value(p) is of (student_t);
```

The treat function can also used to treat a supertype instance as a subtype instance. This is especially useful for assigning a variable to a more specialized type in a hierarchy and accessing attributes or methods of a subtype. As an example, the following query creates a view of student objects. The is of clause is used in the where clause to indicate that the view should include objects of type student_t. The treat function is then used in the select clause to access the attributes that are specific to the student_t object type.

```
create or replace view student(pId, firstName, lastName, dob, status, major,
    memberOf) as
select      pId, firstName, lastName, dob, treat(value(p) as student_t).status,
            treat(value(p) as student_t).major, treat(value(p) as student_t).memberOf
from        person p
where       value(p) is of (student_t);
```

3.9.5 VARRAYS AND NESTED TABLES AS COLLECTIONS

In Oracle, variable-sized arrays (varrays) and nested tables can be used to represent the *many* side of 1: N and M: N relationships.

3.9.5.1 Varrays

Oracle allows arrays to be of a variable size, thus the name varray. A maximum size must be specified when an attribute of type varray is defined. The size can, however, be changed at a later time. To define an attribute as a varray, a varray type definition must first be created. Creating a varray type does not allocate space but simply defines a data type that can be used as the data type of a column of a relational table, an object type attribute, or the type of a PL/SQL variable, parameter, or function return value. In Figure 3.9, the varray type definition of campusClub_array is used to model the *many* side of the advisorOf relationship between campusClub_t and faculty_t. Varray definitions are also shown for student_array and faculty_array, which are used respectably as output in the getStudents and getFaculty functions declared for the department_t object type.

3.9.5.2 Nested Tables

Whereas a varray is an indexed collection of data elements of the same type, a nested table is an unordered set of data elements of the same data type. A nested table has a single column, where the type of the column is a built-in type or an object type. If the column in a nested table is an object type, the table can also be viewed as a multi-column table, with a column for each attribute of the object type. The use of DML statements on nested tables such as select, insert, and delete are the same as with regular relational tables.

In a nested table, the order of the elements is not defined. Nested tables are stored in a storage table with every element mapping to a row in the storage table. Figure 3.9 illustrates a nested table type definition for the student_ntable nested table. The contents of the nested table are of type ref student_t,. The type definition is used to define the members attribute in campusClub_t. The storage table of the members nested table, club_members, is specified in the campusClub table definition. Whereas the programmer accesses the nested table using the name members, the name club_members is used internally by Oracle to access and manipulate the nested table.

Figure 3.9 also shows the use of the scope constraint on the storage table club_members of the members nested table. The constraint indicates that the values stored in the ref column must be references to row objects in the person table. A unique index is created on the storage table club_members using the nested_table_id and column_value columns to restrict the uniqueness of the ref values. The nested_table_id column is a pseudocolumn in nested tables that holds the row identifier of the storage table. The column_value column is a pseudocolumn that holds the contents of the nested table (in this case, a ref of type student_t).

3.9.5.3 Comparison of Varrays and Nested Tables

Varrays and nested tables are similar in that the data types of all elements in each collection must be the same. But varrays and nested tables differ in the way they are internally managed by Oracle. A varray has the following characteristics:

- A varray cannot be indexed.

- A varray declaration must specify the maximum number of objects to hold.

- A varray is dense in that all positions from the first to the last must be filled. Individual elements cannot be deleted from a varray to leave a null value in an array position.

- The elements of a varray are ordered.

- If the size of the varray is smaller than 4000 bytes, Oracle stores the varray in line; if it is greater than 4000 bytes, Oracle stores it in a Binary Large Object (BLOB).

  In comparison, nested tables have the following characteristics:

- A nested table is an unordered set of data elements, all of the same data type having a single column.

- The type of the column in the nested table is either a built-in type or an object type.

- If an object type is used as the type of the column, the table can be viewed as a multi-column table, with a column for each attribute of the object.

- Nested tables are stored in a separate storage table and can be indexed for efficient access.

- Nested tables are sparse (i.e., individual elements can be deleted from a nested table).

The choice between a varray and a nested table depends on the nature of the values or objects stored in the collection. If the number of objects in a multivalued attribute or relationship is large, then a nested table should be used instead of a varray. A varray is normally used when the number of objects contained in a multivalued attribute is small and does not change. Interested readers should consult Oracle 11g documentation for further details about accessing and modifying varrays and nested tables.

3.10 BIBLIOGRAPHIC REFERENCES

In response to the *Object-Oriented Database System Manifesto* prepared by researchers of object-oriented database technology [Atkinson et al., 1990], Michael Stonebraker led a group of researchers in relational database technology in the preparation of the *Third Generation Database System Manifesto*, a document that outlined the manner in which relational technology could be extended to support object-oriented features [Stonebraker et al., 1990]. Rowe and Stonebraker demonstrated the feasibility of object-relational technology with the development of Postgres [Rowe and Stonebraker, 1987], an object-relational version of Ingres [Held et al., 1975] (an early relational database prototype and research tool). Additional sources of information about object-relational technology can be found in [Brown, 2001, Date and Darwen, 1998, Stonebraker, 1995].

The most complete source on the object-relational features of the SQL standard is [Melton, 2002], with additional information about arrays and row types in [Gulutzan and Pelzer, 1999, Melton and Simon, 2001]. The complete SQL standards documents can be ordered by contacting the American National Standards Institute or the International Standards Organization. A description of the object-relational features of Oracle 11g can be found in the Oracle Database Object-Relational Developer's Guide [Oracle, 2010].

The use of the SCHOOL DATABASE ENTERPRISE for mapping to object-relational technology was originally presented in [Urban et al., 2000], with additional mapping issues addressed in [Urban and Dietrich, 2003].

APPENDIX A

Mapping Object-Oriented Conceptual Models to the Relational Data Model

EER and UML diagrams are excellent tools for modeling a database enterprise at a conceptual level. The modeled data and constraints must be mapped to an implementation data model to realize the database application. This appendix reviews the mapping of these object-oriented conceptual models to the relational data model. The mapping coverage emphasizes the importance of maintaining the constraints in the relational data model that are inherent in the object-oriented conceptual models.

The ABSTRACT ENTERPRISE and the HOLLYWOOD ENTERPRISE presented in Chapter 1 form the basis of the mapping discussion. The presentation emphasizes the mapping review using the side-by-side EER and UML diagrams from that chapter.

A.1   NOTATION AND TERMINOLOGY

The mapping of a conceptual model to the relational data model requires using the SQL standard to define relational tables and views for data representation together with constraints that enforce application semantics. Tables and views are different forms of relations. The distinction is that a table is a relation that is explicitly stored in the database, while a view is a relation that is derived using a query specification.

When mapping an object-oriented conceptual model to a relational schema, some components of the conceptual model are mapped to tables while other components are mapped to views. The term *extensional schema* refers to the relations that are defined using the create table statement, whereas the term *intensional schema* refers to the view definitions. For brevity of presentation, this appendix introduces a notation to summarize the specification of the extensional schema. A table definition is summarized by giving the name of the table, listing the attribute names, underlining the attributes that form a candidate key of the table and listing the table constraints. Consider as an example of the notation:

```
tableName(keyAttribute, attr1, attr2, foreignKeyAttr)
     foreign key (foreignKeyAttr) references primaryKeyTable(primaryKeyAttr)
```

This summary schema shows a table named tableName, having four attributes: keyAttribute, attr1, attr2, and foreignKeyAttr. The keyAttribute is a candidate key for the table. The value of a candidate key in a table uniquely identifies a tuple in the table. The foreignKeyAttr is an attribute that references the value of a primary key in another table. Therefore, a referential integrity table constraint is listed as part of the summary definition to capture this constraint in the schema. Since there is only one candidate key for tableName, the candidate key keyAttribute is also the primary key. An explicit primary key table constraint will be used only when a table has more than one candidate key.

If there are multiple candidate keys for a table, each candidate key will be underlined. For example,

tableMultipleCandidateKeys(candidateKey1, anyAttr, candidateKey2)
    primary key candidateKey1

indicates that the table named tableMultipleCandidateKeys has two candidate keys: candidateKey1 and candidateKey2. Each candidate key uniquely identifies a tuple in the table. Therefore, an explicit primary key table constraint indicates which candidate key is considered the primary key for uniquely identifying a row in the table.

If a table has a composite candidate key, then the line underscores all of the attributes that are part of the candidate key. For example,

tableCompositeCandidateKey(partOfCandidateKey1, partOfCandidateKey2, anyAttr)

indicates that the table named tableCompositeCandidateKey has one candidate key that consists of two attributes: partOfCandidateKey1 and partOfCandidateKey2. The value of both attributes is required to uniquely identify a tuple in the table.

In summary, this syntax for describing a table definition is an abbreviation and abstraction to facilitate the presentation of mapping object-oriented conceptual models to the relational data model. This summary syntax is only used for the extensional schema. The view definitions for the intensional schema consist of query definitions, which must be explicitly specified.

A.2   CLASSES

The first step in mapping a conceptual model to the relational data model involves the mapping of classes. This section covers classes that are not part of a class hierarchy, deferring the mapping of class hierarchies to a later section of the appendix.

Consider the class A, shown in Figure 1.3, that has simple attributes (keyOfA, attrOfA), a composite attribute (compositeOfA) and a derived attribute (derivedAttr). Class A is mapped to a table that contains its simple attributes. Since the relational data model does not allow structured types, the composite attribute (compositeOfA) cannot be directly included. However, the simple components (attrA1, attrA2, attrA3) of the composite attribute are included in the table.

a(keyOfA, attrOfA, attrA1, attrA2, attrA3)

The table for A does not include the derived attribute for A. One alternative is to define a view for A, which retrieves the stored attributes and computes the value of the derived attribute (derivedAttr) in the view definition. Another alternative is to explicitly store the value of the derived attribute in the table for A and update its value using triggers, when the value on which it depends changes:

a(<u>keyOfA</u>, attrOfA, attrA1, attrA2, attrA3, derivedAttr)

A classical example of a derived attribute is that of a person's age, which is computed based on the current date and the person's birthdate.

The class C shown in Figure 1.4 has simple attributes (keyOfC, attrOfC) and a multivalued attribute (multiValuedAttr). The class C is mapped to a table of the same name, containing its simple attributes. Since the relational data model allows only simple types for attributes, the multivalued attribute must be mapped to its own table along with the key of the class. The key of the corresponding table (multiC) is a composite key consisting of the key of the class and the multivalued attribute. Note that a referential integrity constraint must hold between the foreign key and the primary key that it references.

c(<u>keyOfC</u>, attrOfC)
multiC(<u>keyOfC, multiValuedAttr</u>)
        foreign key (keyOfC) references c(keyOfC)

A.3   ASSOCIATIONS

The associations of a UML class diagram and the relationships of an EER diagram provide important semantics about the relationships that exist between the entities involved in an enterprise model. These semantics affect the mapping of the conceptual model to relational tables and also determine the constraints that must be expressed to enforce the intended meaning of the associations. This section presents relational mapping considerations for associations. Binary associations can be mapped using either a *bidirectional* or *unidirectional* approach. In a bidirectional mapping, the resulting relational tables can be used to traverse the association in either direction. In a unidirectional association, the mapping only supports traversal of the association in one direction. Although the EER model does not make a distinction between the bidirectional and unidirectional mappings, UML diagrams use navigation to explicitly specify the unidirectional approach.

Mapping techniques must also consider recursive binary associations, n–ary associations, weak entities, class hierarchies, shared subclasses, and categories. All of these features are supported by the EER and the UML modeling techniques. In all cases, participation and multiplicity constraints play an important role in the specification of association constraints. The following sections elaborate on association mappings beginning with mapping techniques for bidirectional binary associations.

A.3.1   BIDIRECTIONAL BINARY ASSOCIATIONS

Using a bidirectional mapping approach, a binary association is mapped to a table, where the attributes of the table include the primary key attributes of the related classes and any descriptive attributes of the association. Since the resulting table representing the binary association contains two foreign keys referencing the primary key attributes of the classes involved in the association, referential integrity constraints must be introduced for each foreign key. The key of the resulting table depends on the multiplicity of the association and the semantics of the enterprise.

The ab association shown in Figure 1.6 represents an M:N relationship between classes A and B. Following the mapping heuristic, the association is mapped to a table containing the key of A (keyOfA), the key of B (keyOfB), and the descriptive attribute of the relationship (attrOfAB). Since ab is an M:N relationship, the key of the table ab is a composite key. If the semantics of the application allow multiple values of attrOfAB for a given (keyOfA, keyOfB) pair, then the key of the ab table is a composite key consisting of the attributes (keyOfA, keyOfB, attrOfAB). If there is exactly one value of attrOfAB for a given (keyOfA, keyOfB) pair, then the primary key of the ab table is (keyOfA, keyOfB), as shown in the following schema.

a(keyOfA, attrOfA, attrA1, attrA2, attrA3)
b(keyOfB, attrOfB)
ab(keyOfA, keyOfB, attrOfAB)
        foreign key (keyOfA) references a(keyOfA),
        foreign key (keyOfB) references b(keyOfB)

The ba association of Figure 1.7 is an example of a 1:N relationship between classes B and A. The mapping of the ba association results in a table named ba containing the attributes keyOfA, keyOfB, and attrOfBA. Since an A is related to exactly one B, the keyOfA forms the primary key of the ba table. The keyOfA and keyOfB attributes are each foreign keys of the ba table. Since an A must be related to an instance of B, there is an additional constraint requiring that the keyOfB attribute is not null. This additional not null constraint is not needed on the table representing the ab association, since the keyOfA and keyOfB attributes are part of the primary key. The value of primary key attributes cannot be null.

a(keyOfA, attrOfA, attrA1, attrA2, attrA3)
b(keyOfB, attrOfB)
ba(keyOfA, keyOfB, attrOfBA)
        foreign key (keyOfA) references a(keyOfA),
        foreign key (keyOfB) references b(keyOfB),
        constraint notNullB not null (keyOfB)

The bc association shown in Figure 1.8 illustrates a 1:1 relationship between classes B and C. Since the BC association does not have any descriptive attributes, its corresponding bc table contains only keyOfB and keyOfC attributes. Each attribute is a candidate key of the bc table based on the 1:1 cardinality ratio, and each attribute is a foreign key. Since B has total participation in the association, indicating that an instance of B must be related to exactly one instance of C, the attribute keyOfB is chosen as the primary key of the bc table. Since keyOfC is a candidate key, additional table constraints are specified to enforce the existence and uniqueness of the attribute.

```
b(keyOfB, attrOfB)
c(keyOfC, attrOfC)
bc(keyOfB, keyOfC)
            primary key (keyOfB),
            foreign key (keyOfB) references b(keyOfB),
            foreign key (keyOfC) references c(keyOfC),
            constraint notNullCandidateKey not null (keyOfC),
            constraint candidateKeyConstraint unique (keyOfC)
```

A.3.2   PARTICIPATION AND MULTIPLICITY CONSTRAINTS

The participation and multiplicity constraints of the advanced conceptual models provide semantics regarding the participation of a class in an association. In the 1:1 bc association, shown in Figure 1.8, class B has total participation in the association, requiring the participation of an instance of class B in the bc association. In the EER diagram, the double line linking class B to the relationship bc indicates total participation. In the UML diagram, the multiplicity of 1..1 on the bc association indicates that an instance of B must be related to a minimum of one and maximum of one instance of C.

In the definition of the bc table, the foreign key and not null constraints on the keyOfC require that a B appearing in the bc table is related to exactly one C. However, these constraints do not check that there is a tuple in the bc table for each tuple in the B table. A schema-level integrity constraint can be used to verify the total participation constraint. For example, the assertion totalBinC verifies the total participation constraint of B in the bc association, checking that there does not exist a B that does not participate in the bc association. Similar schema-level constraints must be specified for the total participation of A in the ab association of Figure 1.6, and the ba association of Figure 1.7.

```
create assertion totalBinBC
    check (not exists
    (select    *
    from       b
    where      b.keyOfB not in
               (select bc.keyOfB
               from bc)));
```

The capability to specify general schema-level constraints is a powerful tool. However, not all implementations of SQL allow for check constraints across multiple tables. An alternative approach to constraint checking is the use of views to find integrity constraint violations. The view notTotalBinBC finds instances of B that do not participate in the bc association.

```
create view notTotalBinBC as
    select    *
    from      b
```

```
where      b.keyOfB not in
           (select bc.keyOfB
           from bc);
```

The min..max multiplicities of UML diagrams and the (min, max) pairs of EER diagrams give specific requirements on the minimum and maximum number of times that an instance of a class participates in an association instance. Consider the abstract EER diagram of Figure A.1. The (2,4) annotating the edge between class D and the relationship de indicates that an instance of class D participates a minimum of 2 times and a maximum of 4 times in the relationship instance. Assume that the class D is mapped to a relational table of the same name containing the primary key keyOfD, and the table de represents the relationship instance containing a composite primary key (keyOfD, keyOfE). The view countDinDE counts the number of times an instance of D participates in the de association. The second operand in the union is required to return a zero count when an instance of D is not participating in the de association.

```
create view countDinDE(keyOfD, countInDE) as
     (select      keyOfD, count(*)
     from         de
     group by keyOfD)
     union
     (select      keyOfD, 0
     from         d
     where        d.keyOfD not in (select de.keyOfD from de));
```

The assertion DinDE verifies the multiplicity constraints using the defined countDinDE view.

```
create assertion DinDE
     check (not exists
     (select      *
     from         countDinDE
     where        countInDE < 2 or countInDE > 4));
```

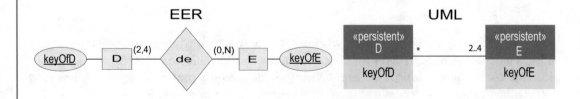

Figure A.1: EER and UML Diagrams Illustrating Minimum and Maximum Constraints

A.3.3   RECURSIVE ASSOCIATIONS

When a binary association relates a class to itself, the association is called a *recursive* association. A canonical example of a recursive binary association is the employee supervisory relationship, since an employee's supervisor is an employee. A recursive association is mapped in the same manner as any other binary association. A table is created with the primary keys of both classes related by the association. Since the primary keys are the same in a recursive association, the names of the attributes in the table representing the association must be renamed to include the role name of the attribute.

As an example, consider the abstract recursive association given in Figure 1.9, which relates the class B to itself via the bb association. The role name parent is given to the one side of the association, and the child role name labels the many side. The table bb that corresponds to the recursive association contains the primary key of B (keyOfB) twice: childKeyOfB and parentKeyOfB. The primary key of the table bb corresponds to the child role in the association (childKeyOfB), since a parent can have many children but a child has one parent.

```
b(keyOfB, attrOfB)
bb(childKeyOfB, parentKeyOfB)
      foreign key (childKeyOfB) references b(keyOfB),
      foreign key (parentKeyOfB) references b(keyOfB)
```

A.3.4   N-ARY ASSOCIATIONS

The most common form of an association is a binary association, which relates two entities. However, associations involving more than two entities are possible. The same mapping approach for binary associations is applicable for associations of degree higher than two. The attributes that form the primary key of each entity involved in the association is included in the resulting table. Any descriptive attributes of the association are also included.

Recall the non-binary finance relationship between Car, Person, and Bank shown in Figure 1.10. The ternary finance relationship represents a car dealership application where a person buys a car that is financed by a specific bank. The finance table representing the ternary association includes the key attributes of all three entities involved in the relationship (inventoryId, pId, and bankId) and the descriptive attribute of the association (loanAmount). The cardinality ratios/multiplicities of the association indicate that the car's inventoryId forms a key for the table, since a car can only be sold once from the dealer's inventory.

```
finance(inventoryId, pId, bankId, loanAmount)
      foreign key (inventoryId) references car(inventoryId),
      foreign key (pId) references person(pId),
      foreign key (bankId) references bank(bankId)
```

A.3.5   NAVIGATION OF UNIDIRECTIONAL ASSOCIATIONS

The bidirectional approach to mapping binary associations presented in Section A.3.1 created a table to represent the relationship containing the primary key attributes of both classes involved in the association. The resulting table provides a mechanism to traverse the association given either of the primary keys of the objects involved in the association. This approach to mapping binary associations assumed that the association was bidirectional. UML diagrams support the concept of navigability that allows the designer to restrict the association to be unidirectional. A unidirectional association indicates that the implementation of the association is only stored in one direction.

Although M:N associations are inherently bidirectional, 1:N and 1:1 associations can be unidirectional and have an alternative mapping approach that does not require creating another table for the association. The alternative mapping strategy stores the primary key of the one-side of the association and any descriptive attributes of the association itself in the table representing the class on the other side of the association.

The UML diagram in Figure 1.12 represents a revision of the UML diagram of Figure 1.2, changing the 1:N ba association to be unidirectional from A to B and the 1:1 bc association to be unidirectional from B to C.

The alternative mapping of the 1:N ba association results in two tables instead of three. Since an A is related to exactly one B, the primary key of the related B (keyOfB) and the descriptive attribute of the ba association (attrOfBA) are included in the table for A. Since A has total participation in the ba association, the keyOfB attribute is constrained to be not null.

> b(keyOfB, attrOfB)
> a(keyOfA, attrOfA, attrA1, attrA2, attrA3, keyOfB, attrOfBA)
>   foreign key (keyOfB) references b(keyOfB),
>   constraint totalParticipationAinBA not null (keyOfB)

A comparison of the schema designs for the mapping of the 1:N ba association is warranted. Since A has total participation in the relationship, the mapping that includes the keyOfB and the attrOfBA in the a table is preferred for performance reasons. When retrieving a tuple from the a table, the information regarding its ba association is accessed at the same time. When the ba association is stored in its own table, the a table and the ba table must be joined to retrieve the same information.

Another performance advantage is realized during database inserts, updates or deletes. When the ba association is stored as part of the table for A, the total participation constraint of A in the ba association is verifiable using a table-level constraint specifying that the keyOfB attribute value cannot be null. When the ba association is stored in its own table, a schema-level constraint is required to enforce the total participation. A table-level constraint is more efficient to enforce than a schema-level constraint.

Another point to notice is that the navigability of an association in the relational data model is not truly affected by the alternative mapping approaches. In both designs, there is a table that contains the primary key attributes of the associated values. The navigability of associations on the resulting schema design is more evident in object-oriented and object-relational approaches.

The alternative unidirectional mapping of the 1:1 bc association also results in two tables instead of three. Since B has total participation in the association, the primary key attributes of C are included in the table for B.

```
c(keyOfC, attrOfC)
b(keyOfB, attrOfB, keyOfC)
            primary key (keyOfB),
            foreign key (keyOfC) references c(keyOfC),
            constraint notNullCandidateKey not null (keyOfC),
            constraint candidateKeyConstraint unique (keyOfC)
```

The unidirectional mapping of the 1:1 bc association shares the same advantages as the unidirectional mapping of the 1:N ba association: the key of the related instance of C is automatically retrieved as part of the tuple for an instance of B, and the total participation of B in the bc association is enforced using the not null table constraint. When neither class has total participation in a 1:1 association, the bidirectional approach is preferred. Without the total participation constraint, there is no clear choice for the direction of the unidirectional association, which results in null values for any instances that do not participate in the 1:1 association.

A.3.6   WEAK ENTITIES AND IDENTIFYING RELATIONSHIPS

The classes that have been mapped up to this point had a primary key, allowing the unique identification of an instance across the entire database. Recall that a weak entity in the EER model is existence dependent on its identifying owner to form a partial key that uniquely identifies the weak entity in the context of its owner. To create a unique identifier for the weak entity, the partial key is combined with the primary key of its identifying owner. A weak entity has total participation in the identifying relationship that links the weak entity to its identifying owner. Figure 1.13 shows the Weak entity of the ABSTRACT ENTERPRISE, having the identifying relationship dependsOn linking to class A as its identifying owner.

The mapping of a weak entity creates a table for that entity with its attributes and the primary key attributes of its identifying owner. The table weak has a composite primary key consisting of the key of its identifying owner (keyOfA) and its partialKey. A referential integrity constraint verifies the validity of the key of the identifying owner.

```
a(keyOfA, attrOfA, attrA1, attrA2, attrA3)
weak(keyOfA, partialKey, attrOfWeak)
            foreign key (keyOfA) references a(keyOfA)
```

When mapping an EER diagram to a relational schema, identifying relationships are not explicitly mapped to a relation since the semantics of the identifying relationship are captured in the mapping of the weak entity itself. Consider as a counter-example the explicit mapping of the dependsOn identifying relationship to its own table. Following the mapping approach for binary associations, the dependsOn table would include the primary key attributes of the identifying owner (A) and the weak entity (Weak). The values of the keyOfA and identifyingKeyOfA attributes would have to be the same. This resulting dependsOn table is redundant in the relational schema since the weak table already captures the identifying owner in the primary key.

dependsOn(<u>keyOfA</u>, <u>partialKey</u>, identifyingKeyOfA)
foreign key (keyOfA) references a(keyOfA),
foreign key (identifyingKeyOfA) references a(keyOfA)

A.3.7   CHECKPOINT: CLASSES AND ASSOCIATIONS

Table A.1 summarizes the heuristics for mapping classes and associations to a relational schema. For each type of component, Table A.1 indicates whether a table is created, the attributes that are added to a table, and the corresponding candidate key. Figure A.2 provides the complete relational schema for the ABSTRACT ENTERPRISE using a unidirectional representation for the navigation of associations as shown in the UML diagram in Figure 1.12. The corresponding EER diagram is shown in Figure 1.1.

Table A.1: Summary of Relational Mapping Heuristics for Classes and Associations.

Component	Table	Attributes	Candidate Key
class C	c	simple attributes of C and the simple components of composite attributes	key of C
multivalued attribute m of C	m	primary key of class C and the attribute m	composite key consisting of the primary key of C in combination with the attribute m
bidirectional (M:N) or n-ary association a	a	primary key of each class involved in the association and the descriptive attributes of a	depends on the multiplicity of a and the semantics of the enterprise
unidirectional association a or bidirectional (1:N and 1:1)	–	add the primary key of the one-side of the association as a foreign key on the other side of the association along with the descriptive attributes of a	candidate key of existing table (in the case of 1:1 association, the foreign key is also a candidate key)
weak entity W	w	primary key of identifying owner class O and the simple attributes of W	composite key consisting of the primary key of O in combination with the partial key of W

A.4   CLASS HIERARCHIES

Object-oriented conceptual models, such as EER and UML diagrams, provide inherent support for class hierarchies, including the inheritance of properties and behavior. The relational data model

```
c(keyOfC, attrOfC)
multiC(keyOfC, multiValuedAttr)
          foreign key(keyOfC) references c(keyOfC)
b(keyOfB, attrOfB, keyOfC, parentKeyOfB)
          primary key (keyOfB),
          foreign key (keyOfC) references c(keyOfC)
          constraint notNullCandidateKey not null (keyOfC),
          constraint candidateKeyConstraint unique (keyOfC)
          /* alter table must be used to establish this recursive reference */
          foreign key (parentKeyOfB) references b(keyOfB)
a(keyOfA, attrOfA, attrOfA, attrA1, attrA2, attrA3, keyOfB, attrOfBA)
          foreign key (keyOfB) references b (keyOfB),
          constraint totalParticipation not null (keyOfB)
ab(keyOfA, keyOfB, attrOfAB)
          foreign key (keyOfA) references a(keyOfA)
          foreign key (keyOfB) references b(keyOfB)
weak(keyOfA, partialKey, attrOfWk)
          foreign key (key OfA) references a(keyOfA)
```

Figure A.2: Relational Schema of ABSTRACT ENTERPRISE using Unidirectional Navigability

provides the concept of a table, which does not inherently support class hierarchies. However, through the use of both the extensional and intensional schemas of the relational data model, class hierarchies can be supported. There are three main approaches for mapping class hierarchies to tables:

1. Creating a table for each class,

2. Creating a table for subclasses only, and

3. Flattening the hierarchy.

The relational schema must represent both the specialized and inherited properties of a class. For each approach, a class C is realized by a relation of the same name, where a relation is either a stored table or a view. Therefore, the relational schema consists of a specification of the extensional schema of stored tables, the intensional schema of views, and the constraints that hold on the relations. The name of a table that is created to assist with the definition of a class will use a suffix to differentiate it from the relation for the class. This discussion uses the HOLLYWOOD ENTERPRISE (see Figures 1.25 and 1.26) as examples of the class hierarchies for the alternative mapping approaches. Section A.4.4 discusses support for specialization constraints.

A.4.1   CREATING A TABLE FOR EACH CLASS

One mapping approach for class hierarchies creates a table for each class in the class hierarchy, including superclasses and subclasses. The table for the superclass contains its attributes. The attributes of the table defined for the subclass include the primary key attributes of its superclass and the specialized attributes of the subclass. A view is defined for the subclass that performs an equijoin of the subclass and superclass tables to include both the inherited and specialized attributes of the subclass.

Consider, as an example, the specialization of Person into the subclasses MovieProfessional and Celebrity in the Hollywood Enterprise. The extensional schema in the relational data model contains a table for Person and a table for each of the subclasses: MovieProfessional and Celebrity. The table names for the subclasses use a suffix of EDB to indicate that the table represents the properties of the subclass that are stored in the extensional database. The primary key and referential integrity constraints specified in the extensional schema enforce the ISA constraint by ensuring that every pId in the movieProfessionalEDB and celebrityEDB tables is a valid pId in the person table.

```
person(pId, gender, name, isMarriedTo, phone, address)
movieProfessionalEDB(pId, company)
        foreign key (pId) references person(pId)
celebrityEDB(pId, agentPId, birthDate)
        foreign key (pId) references person(pId)
```

The relation names that correspond to the subclasses must refer to a relation that provides all of the attributes for a subclass, including its inherited attributes. The movieProfessional and celebrity relations are defined using views to include the inherited attributes of the Person superclass.

```
create view movieProfessional as
    select    p.pId, p.gender, p.name, p.isMarriedTo, p.phone, p.address,
              m.company
    from      person p, movieProfessionalEDB m
    where     p.pId = m.pId;
create view celebrity as
    select    p.pId, p.gender, p.name, p.isMarriedTo, p.phone, p.address,
              c.agentPId, c.birthDate
    from      person p, celebrityEDB c
    where     p.pId = c.pId;
```

A complete representation of the class hierarchies for the Hollywood Enterprise, using the mapping approach where a table is created for each class, is given in Figure A.3 and Figure A.4. The guiding design principle creates a relation for each class that includes both the specialized and inherited attributes. Figure A.3 presents the extensional schema, where the suffix EDB designates the table for a subclass that stores the key of its superclass and its specialized attributes. Figure A.4 provides the view definitions that comprise the intensional schema, assuming the extensional schema of Figure A.3. The view definitions provide the relations that correspond to each subclass, including the inherited attributes.

person(pId, gender, name, isMarriedTo, phone, address)
movieProfessionalEDB(pId, company)
       foreign key (pId) references person(pId)
criticEDB(pId, popularity)
       foreign key (pId) references movieProfessionalEDB(pId)
agentEDB(pId, agentFee)
       foreign key (pId) references movieProfessionalEDB(pId)
celebrityEDB(pId, agentpId, birthDate)
       foreign key (pId) references person(pId)
       foreign key (agentpId) references agentEDB(pId)
movieStarEDB(pId, movieType)
       foreign key (pId) references celebrityEDB(pId)
modelEDB(pId, preferences)
       foreign key (pId) references celebrityEDB(pId)
project(projectId, cost, type, location)
filmProjectEDB(projectId, title)
       foreign key (projectId) references project(projectId)
modelingProjectEDB(projectId, description)
       foreign key (projectId) references project(projectId)
actsIn(movieStarPId, filmProjectId)
       foreign key (movieStarPId) references movieStarEDB(pId)
       foreign key (filmProjectId)
       references filmProjectEDB(projectId)
modelsIn(modelPId, modelingProjectId, paid)
       foreign key (modelPId) references modelEDB(pId)
       foreign key (modelingProjectId)
       references modelingProjectEDB(projectId)

Figure A.3: Extensional Schema for Class Hierarchies of the HOLLYWOOD ENTERPRISE

A.4.2   CREATING A TABLE FOR SUBCLASSES ONLY

Another approach to mapping a class hierarchy to a relational schema creates a table for each subclass in the class hierarchy. In this approach, the table for each subclass includes both the specialized and inherited attributes. The relation for a superclass is defined using a view as a generalization of its subclasses. The view inherently supports the ISA constraint, requiring that the subclass is a superclass.

Consider the specialization of Project into a FilmProject or ModelingProject. Since the table for the subclass includes all of the attributes for the subclass, including the inherited ones, the names of the tables for the subclasses are filmProject and modelingProject.

filmProject(projectId, title, cost, type, location)

```
create view movieProfessional as
    select      p.pId, p.gender, p.name, p.isMarriedTo, p.phone, p.address,
                m.company
    from        person p natural join movieProfessionalEDB m;
create view critic as
    select      m.pId, m.gender, m.name, m.isMarriedTo, m.phone, m.address,
                m.company, c.popularity
    from        movieProfessional m natural join criticEDB c;
create view agent as
    select      m.pId, m.gender, m.name, m.isMarriedTo, m.phone, m.address,
                m.company, a.agentFee
    from        movieProfessional m natural join agentEDB a;
create view celebrity as
    select      p.pId, p.gender, p.name, p.isMarriedTo, p.phone, p.address,
                c.agent, c.birthDate
    from        person p natural join celebrityEDB c;
create view filmProject as
    select      p.projectId, p.location, p.cost, p.type, f.title
    from        project p natural join filmProjectEDB f
    where       p.type = 'F';
create view modelingProject as
    select      p.projectId, p.location, p.cost, p.type, m.description
    from        project p natural join modelingProjectEDB m
    where       p.type = 'M';
```

Figure A.4: Intensional Schema for Class Hierarchies of the HOLLYWOOD ENTERPRISE

modelingProject(projectId, description, cost, type, location)

The relation for the Project superclass is defined by a view that is a union of the inherited attributes from the filmProject and modelingProject tables. Therefore, the ISA constraint of the hierarchy, indicating that a FilmProject is a Project and a ModelingProject is a Project, is inherently supported by the intensional schema.

```
create view project as
select      projectId, cost, type, location
from        filmProject
union
select      projectId, cost, type, location
from        modelingProject;
```

In mapping a class hierarchy via the approach in which a table is created for subclasses only, there are several issues to consider. One issue is that this mapping approach cannot support a partial specialization since there is no explicit representation of the superclass in the extensional database. Another issue is based on specializations that are not disjoint. If the specialization is overlapping, then the inherited attributes are stored redundantly in each subclass. As a result, this mapping approach should be used for specializations that are both disjoint and total.

A.4.3   FLATTENING THE HIERARCHY

The third approach to mapping a class hierarchy is to *flatten the hierarchy* into a single table. The table includes the attributes of the superclass and each subclass, and includes type fields to indicate the subclasses to which a tuple belongs. Thus, the ISA constraint is inherently supported. If a tuple in the table does not belong to a subclass, then the corresponding specific attributes of the specialization have null values. This approach is not recommended if there are many attributes for the specialized subclasses.

Again, consider the mapping of the MovieProfessional specialization into Critic and Agent subclasses. Throughout all mapping approaches, a relation name that corresponds to a class C represents the specialized and inherited attributes of the class. Mapping the MovieProfessional hierarchy into a flattened table requires the introduction of a table in the extensional database to maintain all attributes of the hierarchy. In this example, the suffix Hierarchy indicates that the stored table mpCriticAgentHierarchy represents the entire hierarchy. The pId attribute describes the primary key for the relation. The company attribute is the only specialized attribute of a MovieProfessional. The popularity attribute is a specialized attribute of Critic, and the agentFee attribute is a specialized property of an Agent. The subtype attribute indicates whether the MovieProfessional is a Critic or an Agent.

mpCriticAgentHierarchy(pId, company, popularity, agentFee, subtype)

The intensional schema provides the mapping for each class from the MovieProfessional hierarchy. These views assume the same design principle that there exists a relation named person that describes the attributes of the Person class. Therefore, the relations for the MovieProfessional, Critic and Agent classes must include the inherited attributes from Person.

```
create view movieProfessional as
        select      p.pId, p.gender, p.name, p.address, p.isMarriedTo,
                    p.phone, h.company
        from        person p natural join mpCriticAgentHierarchy h;
create view critic as
        select      m.pId, m.gender, m.name, m.address, m.isMarriedTo,
                    m.phone, m.company, h.popularity
        from        movieProfessional m natural join mpCriticAgentHierarchy h
        where       h.subtype = 'c';
create view agent as
        select      m.pId, m.gender, m.name, m.address, m.isMarriedTo,
                    m.phone, m.company, h.agentFee
```

```
from       movieProfessional m natural join mpCriticAgentHierarchy h
where      h.subtype = 'a';
```

Since the specialization of MovieProfessional into the Critic and Agent subclasses is disjoint, the specification of the corresponding subclasses uses a single type indicator (subtype). Multiple type indicators can be used to specify overlapping subclasses. Consider the Celebrity specialization into the overlapping subclasses of MovieStar and Model. Again, the suffix Hierarchy is appended to the table name, representing that the celebrityHierarchy table is a flattening of the Celebrity hierarchy. The pId attribute forms the primary key of the resulting table. The birthDate and agentPId attributes are the specialized properties for a Celebrity. A MovieStar has an additional attribute for movieType, and a Model has an additional attribute for preferences. The Boolean attributes movieStar and model indicate membership of the Celebrity in the corresponding subclass.

celebrityHierarchy(pId, birthDate, agentPId, movieStar, movieType, model, preferences)

The intensional schema defines relations for Celebrity, MovieStar and Model, assuming an existing person relation that describes the attributes of the Person class. Since Celebrity is a subclass of Person and the MovieStar and Model are subclasses of Celebrity, they all inherit the attributes of Person.

```
create view celebrity as
        select     p.pId, p.gender, p.name, p.address, p.isMarriedTo, p.phone,
                   h.birthDate, h.agentPId
        from       person p natural join celebrityHierarchy h;
create view movieStar as
        select     c.pId, c.gender, c.name, c.address, c.isMarriedTo, c.phone,
                   c.birthDate, c.agentPId, h.movieType
        from       celebrity c natural join celebrityHierarchy h
        where      h.movieStar;
create view model as
        select     c.pId, c.gender, c.name, c.address, c.isMarriedTo, c.phone,
                   c.birthDate, c.agentPId, h.preferences
        from       celebrity c natural join celebrityHierarchy h
        where      h.model;
```

Attribute-defined subclasses are inherently supported using a single type indicator when flattening the hierarchy. Consider again the attribute-defined specialization of Project into a FilmProject or a ModelingProject. When the hierarchy is flattened, the extensional schema consists of one table named projectHierarchy. Again, the Hierarchy suffix indicates that this table represents the flattened hierarchy and not the Project class itself. All projects have the attributes projectId, location, cost, and type, where the type field indicates the type of the project. A FilmProject has a specialized attribute title, and the attribute description is a specialized attribute of ModelingProject.

projectHierarchy(projectId, location, cost, type, title, description)

The intensional schema provides a relation for each class (Project, FilmProject and ModelingProject) in the hierarchy using a view definition to provide the appropriate attributes of each class.

```
create view project as
        select      h.projectId, h.location, h.cost, h.type
        from        projectHierarchy h;
create view filmProject as
        select      h.projectId, h.location, h.cost, h.type, h.title
        from        projectHierarchy h
        where       h.type = 'F';
create view modelingProject as
        select      h.projectId, h.location, h.cost, h.type, h.description
        from        projectHierarchy h
        where       h.type = 'M';
```

A.4.4   SPECIALIZATION CONSTRAINTS

As illustrated in Chapter 1, EER and UML diagrams provide inherent support for several specialization constraints: disjoint, completeness, and attribute-defined. The disjoint constraint specifies whether the subclasses in the resulting specialization are disjoint or overlapping. The completeness constraint indicates whether the specialization is total or partial. A total specialization requires that the superclass must participate in the specialization into one of its subclasses. The attribute-defined specialization constraint requires that the value of an attribute on which the specialization is defined is of the appropriate value for the subclass. These specialization constraints are not inherently supported by the relational model but can be specified using schema-level integrity constraints. This exposition leverages the guiding principle in the design of the relational schema that realizes a class C by a relation of the same name. Whether a relation is defined as a stored table or a view is transparent in the constraint specifications.

Consider the specification of the disjoint constraint disjointPersonSpecialization asserting the disjoint specialization of Person into MovieProfessional and Celebrity. The disjoint constraint is violated if the pId of a Person represents both a MovieProfessional and a Celebrity.

```
create assertion disjointPersonSpecialization as
    check (not exists
    (select     *
    from        person p
    where       p.pId in (select m.pId from movieProfessional m) and
                p.pId in (select c.pId from celebrity c)));
```

In the HOLLYWOOD ENTERPRISE, a MovieProfessional has a total specialization into a Critic or Agent, requiring that a MovieProfessional is either a Critic or an Agent. The total specialization constraint is violated if the pId of a MovieProfessional does not appear in the relations for Critic or Agent.

```
create assertion totalMovieProfessionalSpecialization as
    check (not exists
    (select     *
    from        movieProfessional m
    where       m.pId not in
                (select c.pId from critic c union select a.pId from agent a)));
```

The attribute-defined specialization constraint requires that the value of the attribute type of a Project is either 'F' for a FilmProject or 'M' for a ModelingProject.

```
create assertion attrDefinedFilmProjectSpecialization as
    check (not exists
    (select     *
    from        project p
    where       (p.projectId in (select f.projectId from filmProject f) and
                p.type <> 'F') or
                (p.projectId not in (select f.projectId from filmProject f) and
                p.type = 'F')));
```

The attribute-defined specialization constraint is violated if the projectId attribute is considered a FilmProject and the type attribute is not 'F' or if the type attribute is 'F' and the projectId attribute does not represent a FilmProject. A companion constraint must also be included to verify the value of the type attribute for a ModelingProject.

A summary of the specialization constraints in the alternative mapping approaches for mapping class hierarchies is given in Table A.2. A checkmark indicates that the mapping approach can satisfy the constraint, whereas an X indicates that the mapping approach should not be used for the indicated specialization constraint. A comment in parentheses provides a brief indication of how the approach supports or fails to support the specialization constraint. A summary of the specialization constraints supported by each approach as indicated in Table A.2 follows:

- Creating a table for each class
  This mapping approach allows for the support of disjoint or overlapping specializations, total or partial specializations, and attribute-defined specializations.

- Creating a table for subclasses only
  This approach supports disjoint and total specializations, which includes attribute-defined specializations. Overlapping specializations would result in redundancy of the inherited attributes of the superclass, which are stored in the table for each subclass. A partial specialization is not supported because the superclass is represented as a union of the inherited attributes stored in the tables for the subclasses.

- Flattening the hierarchy
This mapping design also allows for the support of disjoint or overlapping specializations, total or partial specializations, and attribute-defined specializations. A single type indicator represents a disjoint specialization since the attribute is single-valued. Overlapping specializations are represented using multiple type indicators. Partial specializations are allowed. If the superclass does not belong to a subclass, then the values of all of the specialized attributes would be null.

Mapping Approach	Disjoint Constraint		Completeness Constraint		Attribute-defined
	Disjoint	Overlapping	Total	Partial	
Table for each class	✓	✓	✓	✓	✓
Table for each subclass	✓	✗ (redundancy)	✓	✗ (no superclass)	✓
Flattening the hierarchy	✓ (single type indicator)	✓ (multiple type indicators)	✓	✓ (null values)	✓

Table A.2: Summary of Support for Specialization Constraints for Mapping Class Hierarchies.

A.4.5   CHECKPOINT: CLASS HIERARCHIES

Table A.3 provides a summary of the approaches for mapping class hierarchies using the simple, abstract hierarchy shown in Figure A.5, consisting of a superclass S and two subclasses S1 and S2. The extensional database (EDB) row provides a summary of the table definitions. The intensional database (IDB) row gives a summary of the view definitions.

Figure A.6 provides a template of the SQL assertion statements needed to support the specification of the specialization constraints for disjoint specializations, total specializations, and attribute-defined specializations. The template assumes the class superclass with primary key keyOfS has a specialization into two subclasses: subclass1 and subclass2. The attribute-defined specialization constraint requires a constraint for each subclass. Figure A.6 shows the attribute-defined specialization constraint for the S1 subclass. The companion constraint for the S2 subclass is not shown.

A.5   SHARED SUBCLASSES

A shared subclass is a class that has more than one superclass organized in a specialization lattice. Figure 1.21 illustrates an example of the StarModel shared subclass that is both a MovieStar and

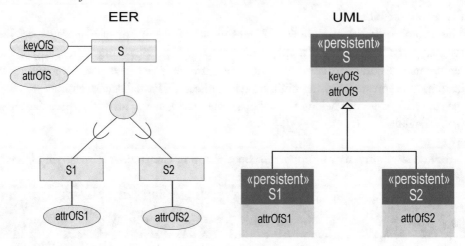

Figure A.5: EER and UML Diagrams for a Simple Class Hierarchy

```
create assertion disjointSpecialization as
    check (not exists
    (select     *
    from       superclass S
    where      S.keyOfS in (select S1.keyOfS from subclass1 S1) and
               S.keyOfS in (select S2.keyOfS from subclass2 S2)));
create assertion totalSpecialization as
    check (not exists
    (select     *
    from       superclass S
    where      S.keyOfS not in
               (select S1.keyOfS from subclass1 S1
               union
               select S2.keyOfS from subclass2 S2)));
create assertion attrDefinedSpecializationS1 as
    check (not exists
    (select     *
    from       superclass S
    where      (S.keyOfS in (select S1.keyOfS from subclass1 S1) and
               S.type <> 'S1')
               or
               (S.keyOfS not in (select S1.keyOfS from subclass1 S1) and
               S.type = 'S1')));
```

Figure A.6: SQL Assertion Specification Template for Specialization Constraints

Table A.3: Summary of Relational Mapping Heuristics for Class Hierarchies.

Create a table for each class	
EDB	s(keyOfS, attrOfS)
	s1EDB(keyOfS, attrOfS1)
	foreign key(keyOfS) references s(keyOfS)
	s2EDB(keyOfS, attrOfS2)
	foreign key(keyOfS) references s(keyOfS)
IDB	create view s1 as select * from s natural join s1EDB
	create view s2 as select * from s natural join s2EDB
Create a table for subclasses only	
EDB	s1(keyOfS, attrOfS1)
	s2(keyOfS, attrOfS2)
IDB	create view s as (select keyOfS, attrOfS from s1)
	union (select keyOfS, attOfS from s2)
Flattening the hierarchy (single type indicator)	
EDB	sHierarchy(keyOfS, attrOfS, attrOfS1, attrOfS2, type)
IDB	create view s as select keyOfS, attrOfS from sHierarchy
	create view s1 as
	select keyOfS, attrOfS, attrOfS1 from sHierarchy where type='S1'
	create view s2 as
	select keyOfS, attrOfS, attrOfS2 from sHierarchy where type='S2'
Flattening the hierarchy (multiple type indicators)	
EDB	sHierarchy(keyOfS, attrOfS, typeS1, attrOfS1, typeS2, attrOfS2)
IDB	create view s as select keyOfS, attrOfS from sHierarchy
	create view s1 as
	select keyOfS, attrOfS, attrOfS1 from sHierarchy where typeS1=TRUE
	create view s2 as
	select keyOfS, attrOfS, attrOfS2 from sHierarchy where typeS2=TRUE

Model. If the superclasses have a common ancestor, then the shared subclass has the same key attribute and several of the mapping approaches of the class hierarchy are possible. For example, consider mapping the Celebrity class hierarchy using the table for each class approach. The extensional database consists of a table for each class:

```
person(pId, gender, name, isMarriedTo, phone, address)
celebrityEDB(pId, birthDate)
movieStarEDB(pId, movieType)
modelEDB(pId, preferences)
starModelEDB(pId)
```

To support the appropriate inherited attributes, the intensional schema defines views for Celebrity, MovieStar, Model, and StarModel. For brevity, only the StarModel view is shown.

```
create view starModel as
        select      c.pId, c.gender, c.name, c.isMarriedTo, c.phone,
                    c.address c.birthDate, ms.movieType, m.preferences
        from        (((starModelEDB s natural join modelEDB m)
                    natural join movieStarEDB ms)
                    natural join celebrity c);
```

If the hierarchy is flattened, then the extensional schema consists of the celebrityHierarchy table.

```
celebrityHierarchy(pId, birthDate, movieStar, movieType, model, preferences)
```

The intensional schema defines the starModel view based on both Boolean attributes movieStar and model being TRUE. Note that this view assumes the relation celebrity is already defined, containing all of the attributes describing the Celebrity class.

```
create view starModel as
        select      c.pId, c.gender, c.name, c.isMarriedTo, c.phone,
                    c.address, c.birthDate, h.movieType, h.preferences
        from        celebrity c join celebrityHierarchy h
        where       h.movieStar and h.model;
```

Since the mapping approach that creates a table for subclasses only requires a disjoint and total specialization, this mapping approach is not applicable to shared subclasses that are inherently overlapping and partial specializations.

A.6   CATEGORIES

A category in the EER or the Xor constraint in UML requires the introduction of a *surrogate key* attribute for mapping to the relational data model. The surrogate key represents a mechanism for the database system to generate a unique value for a category, which models a union of two or more different types of classes having different primary key attributes. For the Sponsor category of Figure 1.23 and the Sponsor Xor constraint of Figure 1.24, a table is created for the Sponsor category containing the surrogate key attribute sponsorCode. The sponsorCode surrogate key is also an attribute of each of the tables for the unioned superclasses person and company. Since there is only one sponsor for a modeling project, the surrogate key sponsorCode is included in the modelingProjectEDB table to identify the sponsor of the project.

```
sponsor (sponsorCode)
person (pId, name, phone, gender, address, sponsorCode)
        foreign key (sponsorCode) references sponsor(sponsorCode)
company (cId, cName, sponsorCode)
```

```
            foreign key (sponsorCode) references sponsor(sponsorCode)
modelingProjectEDB (projectId, description, sponsorCode)
            foreign key (projectId) references project (projectId)
            foreign key (sponsorCode) references sponsor(sponsorCode)
```

Since a category represents the union of its superclasses, a schema-level assertion enforces that the surrogate key appears in one of the superclasses:

```
create assertion sponsorCategoryUnion
check (not exists
        (select    *
        from       sponsor s
        where      s.sponsorCode not in
                   (select   p.sponsorCode
                   from      person p
                   union
                   select    c.sponsorCode
                   from      company c)));
```

A category is also an exclusive-or of its superclasses as shown in the UML diagram of Figure 1.24. Another schema-level constraint for a category checks that a surrogate key value is not in more than one superclass:

```
create assertion sponsorCategoryXor
check (not exists
        (select    *
        from       sponsor s
        where      s.sponsorCode in
                   (select   p.sponsorCode
                   from      person p
                   intersect
                   select    c.sponsorCode
                   from      company c)));
```

If a category is constrained to be total, then every instance of each superclass must participate in the categorization and be an instance of the category subclass. To enforce the total categorization constraint, add a constraint requiring that the surrogate key attribute in each superclass table is not null.

```
sponsor (sponsorCode)
person (pId, name, phone, gender, address, sponsorCode)
        foreign key (sponsorCode) references sponsor(sponsorCode)
        constraint totalPerson not null (sponsorCode)
company (cId, cName, sponsorCode)
        foreign key (sponsorCode) references sponsor(sponsorCode)
```

constraint totalCompany not null (sponsorCode)

A.7   CHECKPOINT

The mapping of the semantic constructs of the object-oriented conceptual models to the relational data model consists of three parts: an extensional schema of stored tables (including column and table-level constraints), an intensional schema of view definitions, and the schema-level constraints that provide the semantic checking of the relations.

The mapping of classes, attributes, and associations emphasized how the constraints inherent in the conceptual model can be realized in the corresponding mapping to the relational data model. Bidirectional associations of M:N, 1:N, and 1:1 cardinality ratios mapped to tables consisting of the primary key attributes of both classes involved in the association and any descriptive attributes of the association. The referential integrity constraints are enforced by the specification of foreign keys in the schema definition. The enforcement of participation and multiple constraints were also discussed as well as recursive associations, n-ary associations, identifying relationships, and the navigability of associations.

The mapping of class hierarchies covered three approaches:

1. Creating a table for each class,

2. Creating a table for subclasses only, and

3. Flattening the hierarchy.

The guiding design principle of the mapping of the class hierarchies mapped a class C to a relation of the same name containing all the attributes that describe the class, including both specialized and inherited attributes. The relation for a class could be stored as a table as part of the extensional schema or as a view as part of the intensional schema. The naming convention for class relations allowed the reuse of the templates for verifying specialization constraints (disjoint, total, and attribute-defined) across all three mapping approaches.

The appendix concluded with a discussion of the mapping of shared subclasses and categories. Several schema-level constraints are necessary to enforce the constraints inherent in a categorization as the (exclusive) union of its superclasses.

A.8   BIBLIOGRAPHIC REFERENCES

The *extensional* and *intensional* database terminology is from the research area known as deductive databases, which investigated logic programming languages as database query languages [Ramakrishnan and Ullman, 1995]. Most deductive database prototypes used facts to store the extensional database and rules to define the intensional database. The mapping of object-oriented conceptual data models to the relational data model given in this chapter is a synergy of the myriad approaches presented in the deductive database literature, other database text-books [Elmasri and Navathe, 2010], and the semantic data modeling research.

The mapping of the object-oriented conceptual models to the relational model also forms the basis for understanding object relational mapping (ORM) tools. ORMs provide an object view of relational data. The use of ORMs is driven by the need of today's applications, which are written in OOPLs, that must access data stored in a relational database. ORMs provide a higher level of abstraction for an OOPL to access relational data over the use of a call-level interface in which an API is used to query the relational database and process the result set. In an ORM, annotations or configuration specifications assist in the mapping between relations and objects. There are several ORMs available including the Java Persistence API [Yang, 2010] and the Hibernate [Bauer and King, 2006] open-source implementation, which has a corresponding NHibernate [Kuate et al., 2009] for the .NET Framework. Some ORMs also provide support for the generation of the relational schema from the object schema. Hibernate supports three strategies for mapping inheritance: table per class hierarchy, table per subclass, and table per concrete class. Additional mappings involving the union and join of subclasses are possible.

In Chapter 2, the LINQ language was presented as an object query language for OODBs. LINQ also provides querying capabilities over collections of relational tuples using LINQ to SQL [Calvert and Kulkarni, 2009], which is an ORM since it provides an object view of relational data.

Bibliography

J. Albahari. LINQPad, 2010. http://www.linqpad.net 64

K. Arnold, J. Gosling, and D. Holmes. *The Java(TM) Programming Language (4th Edition)*, Addison-Wesley, 2005. 28

M. Atkinson, F. Bancilhon, D. DeWitt, K. Dittrich, D. Maier, and S. Zdonik. The object-oriented database system manifesto. In *Proc. of the 1st Int. Conf. on Deductive and Object-Oriented Databases*, Kyoto, Japan. Elsevier Science Publishers B.V (NorthHolland), 1990. 27, 114

C. Bauer and G. King. *Java Persistence with Hibernate*, Manning, 2006. 139

G. Booch. *Object-Oriented Analysis and Design with Applications*, Second Edition, Benjamin/Cummings Publishers, Redwood City, California, 1994. 30

P. Brown. *Object-Relational Database Development: a Plumber's Guide*, Prentice Hall, Inc., Upper Saddle River, New Jersey, 2001. 114

C. Calvert and D. Kulkarni. *Essential LINQ*, Addison-Wesley Professional, 2009. 64, 139

R. G. G. Cattell,, D. K. Barry, M. Berler, J. Eastman, D. Jordan, C. Russell, O. Schadow, T. Stanienda, and F. Velez (editors). *The Object Data Standard: ODMG 3.0*, Morgan Kaufmann, 2000. 64

A. Chaudhri and R. Zicari (editors). *Succeeding with Object Databases: A Practical Look at Today's Implementations with Java and XML*, J. Wiley, 2000. 64, 144

P. Chen. The Entity Relationship Model - Toward a Unified View of Data. In *Transactions on Database Systems*, vol. 1, no. 1, March 1976. DOI: 10.1145/320434.320440 27

O.-J. Dahl, B. Myhrhaug, and K. Nygaard. *Simula 67 Common Base Language*, Norwegian Computer Center, Oslo, Norway, 1967. 27

C. J. Date and H. Darwen. *Foundations for Object/Relational Databases: The Third Manifesto*, Addison-Wesley, Menlo Park, California, 1998. 114

S. W. Dietrich and M. Chaudhari. The Missing LINQ between Databases and Object-Oriented Programming: LINQ as an Object Query Language for a Database Course. *Journal of Computing in Small Colleges*, Volume 24, Number 4, pages 282-288, 2009. 64

S. Edlich, H. Hörning, R. Hörning, and J. Paterson. *The Definitive Guide to db4o*, Apress, 2006. 64

R. Elmasri and S. Navathe. *Fundamentals of Database Systems*, Sixth Edition, Addison-Wesley, Reading, Massachusetts, 2010. 27, 139

R. Elmasri, J. Weeldreyer, and A. Hevner. The Category Concept: An Extension to the Entity Relationship Model. *International Journal on Data and Knowledge Engineering*, vol. 1, no. 1, May 1985. DOI: 10.1016/0169-023X(85)90027-8 27

R. Elmasri and G. Wiederhold. Structural Properties of Relationships and their Representations. In *Proceedings of the National Computer Conference*, AFIPS, volume 49, 1980. DOI: 10.1109/AFIPS.1980.87 27

M. Fowler. *UML Distilled: A Brief Guide to the Standard Object Modeling Language* (3rd Edition), Addison-Wesley Publishers, 2003. 30

A. Goldberg and D. Robson. *Smalltalk-80: The Language and Its Implementation*, Addison-Wesley Publishers, Reading, Massachusetts, 1983. 27

P. Gulutzan and T. Pelzer. *SQL-99 Complete Really!*, Miller Freeman, Lawrence, Kansas, 1999. 114

G. Held, M. Stonebraker, and E. Wong. Ingres - A Relational Database System. In *Proceedings of the AFIPS National Computer Conference*, pages 409-416, 1975. 114

R. Hull and R. King. Semantic Data Modeling: Survey, Applications, and Research Issues. In *ACM Computing Surveys*, vol. 19, no. 3, September, 1987. DOI: 10.1145/45072.45073 27

I. Jacobson, M. Christerson, P. Jonsson, and G. Overgaard. *Object-Oriented Software Engineering: A Use Case Driven Approach*, Addison-Wesley Publishers, Wokingham, England, 1992. 28

S. Koshafian and G. Copeland. Object Identity. In *Readings in Object-Oriented Database Systems*, S. Zdonik and D. Maier (editors), Morgan Kaufmann, 1989. 27

P. H. Kuate, C. Bauer, G. King, and T.Harris. *NHibernate in Action*, Manning, 2009. 139

M. E. S. Loomis and A. Chaudhri (editors). *Object Databases in Practice*, Prentice Hall, 1997. 64

F. Marguerie, S. Eichert, and J. Wooley. *LINQ in Action*, Manning, 2008. 64

J. Melton and A. Simon. *SQL:1999 Understanding Relational Language Components*, Morgan Kaufmann Publishers, San Francisco, California, 2001. 114

J. Melton. *Advanced SQL:1999 Understanding Object-Relational and Other Advance Features*, Morgan Kaufmann Publishers, San Francisco, California, 2002. 114

B. Meyer. *Object-Oriented Software Construction*, Prentice Hall Publishers, New York, New York, 1988. 27

R. Muller. *Database Design for Smarties: Using UML for Data Modeling*, Morgan Kaufmann Publishers, San Francisco, California, 1999. 30

ODBMS.ORG Object Database Management Systems: The Resource Portal for Education and Research, R. Zicari (editor), `http://odbms.org` 64

OMG Unified Modeling Language Specification, Version 2.3, Object Management Group, May 2010, `http://www.omg.org/spec/UML/`. 30

Oracle Database Object-Relational Developers Guide, `http://download.oracle.com/docs/cd/B28359_01/appdev.111/b28371/adobjint.htm`. 114

J. Peckham and F. Maryanski. Semantic Data Models. In *ACM Computing Surveys*, vol. 20, no. 3, pages 153-189, 1988. DOI: 10.1145/62061.62062 27

R. Ramakrishnan and J. Ullman. A Survey of Deductive Databases. *Journal Of Logic Programming*, vol. 23, no. 2, pages 125-149, 1995. DOI: 10.1016/0743-1066(94)00039-9 138

L. Rowe and M. Stonebraker. The Postgres Data Model. In *Proceedings of the Thirteenth International Conference on Very Large Data Bases*, Brighton, England, pages 83-96, 1987. 114

J. Rumbaugh, M. Blaha, W. Premerlani, F. Eddy, and W. Lorensen. *Object-Oriented Modeling and Design*, Prentice Hall Publishers, Englewood Cliffs, New Jersey, 1991. 28

J. Rumbaugh, I. Jacobson, and G. Booch. *The Unified Modeling Language Reference Manual (2nd Edition)*, Addison-Wesley, Upper Saddle River, New Jersey, 2004. 30

J. Schmuller. *Sams Teach Yourself UML in 24 Hours* (3rd Edition), SAMS Publishing, Indianapolis, Indiana, 2004. 30

J. Smith and D. Smith. Database Abstractions: Aggregation and Generalization. In *Transactions on Database Systems*, vol. 2, no. 2, June 1977. DOI: 10.1145/320544.320546 27

M. Stonebraker, L. Rowe, B. Lindsay, J. Gray, M. Carey, M. Brodie, P. Bernstein, and D. Beech. Third Generation Database System Manifesto. In *SIGMOD Record*, vol. 19, no. 3, pages 31-44, 1990. DOI: 10.1145/101077.390001 114

M. Stonebraker, *Object-Relational DBMSs: The Next Great Wave*, Morgan Kaufmann, San Francisco, California, 1995. 114

B. Stroustrup. *The C++ Programming Language*, 1st Edition, Addison-Wesley, 1986. 27

B. Stroustrup. *The C++ Programming Language*, Special Edition, Addison-Wesley, 2000. 28

S. D. Urban. Database Models. In *Encyclopedia of Electrical and Electronics Engineering*, John G. Webster (editor), John Wiley & Sons, Inc., vol. 4, pages 604-629, 1999. 30

S. D. Urban, S. W. Dietrich, and P. Tapia. Mapping UML Diagrams to Object-Relational Schemas in Oracle 8. In [Chaudhri and Zicari, 2000]. 114

S. D. Urban and S. W. Dietrich. Using UML Class Diagrams for a Comparative Analysis of Relational, Object-Oriented, and Object-Relational Database Mappings. In *ACM SIGCSE International Conference on Computer Science Education*, Reno, Nevada, February, 2003. DOI: 10.1145/792548.611923 114

Versant, db4o, http://www.db4o.com 64

G. Wiederhold and R. Elmasri. The Structural Model for Database Design. In *Proceedings of the Entity Relationship Conference*, 1979. 27

D. Yang. *Java Persistence with JPA*, Outskirts Press, 2010. 139

Authors' Biographies

SUZANNE W. DIETRICH

Suzanne W. Dietrich is an associate professor in the Applied Computing program within the Division of Mathematical and Natural Sciences at Arizona State University. Her research interests include database query languages, data modeling, and computer science education. Dr. Dietrich's research has been supported by grants from the National Science Foundation, including the maintenance of materialized views over heterogeneous structured data sources in a distributed environment with events and streams; the integration of declarative, object, and active features for distributed multitiered applications; and the development of novel approaches to undergraduate database education. She is recognized by the ACM as a Distinguished Educator and is the author of *Understanding Relational Database Query Languages* (Prentice Hall 2001).

SUSAN D. URBAN

Susan D. Urban is a professor in the Department of Computer Science at Texas Tech University. Her research interests include data and process modeling as well as integrated techniques for event, rule, and transaction processing to address data consistency and active behavior in distributed, data-centric applications. Dr. Urban has been the recipient of several grants from the National Science Foundation for her research on constraints, active rule processing in centralized and distributed environments, data consistency issues in service-oriented environments, the use of databases in engineering design, and the development of innovative teaching concepts for database instruction. She has published over 100 refereed papers and book chapters on the results of her research.

Index

Printed in the United States
by Baker & Taylor Publisher Services